JACK THE
RIPPER
THE
TERRIBLE LEGACY

THE WHITECHAPEL SOCIETY

JACK THE RIPPER

THE TERRIBLE LEGACY

THE WHITECHAPEL SOCIETY

The History Press

First published 2013

The History Press
The Mill, Brimscombe Port
Stroud, Gloucestershire, GL5 2QG
www.thehistorypress.co.uk

British Library Cataloguing in Publication Data.
A catalogue record for this book is available from the British Library.

ISBN 978 0 7524 9331 2

Typesetting and origination by The History Press
Printed and bound in Great Britain by
Marston Book Services Limited, Oxfordshire

Contents

Acknowledgements

The Whitechapel Society gratefully acknowledges the following for the material and the assistance they have provided: The Bancroft Library; The Bishopsgate Institute; British Library Newspapers; The National Archives; www.casebook.org; www.jtrforums.com; Mark Galloway; Richard Nash; Robin Odell; Peter Leyland; Alyn Smith; Richard Clarke; Nicholas Connell; Ted Ball; Roger Palmer and Stewart P. Evans.
A special thank you to our members for their continued support.

The opinions expressed in this publication are those of the individual authors and do not represent the Whitechapel Society as a whole.

Introduction

By Robin Odell

The eighteenth-century English poet Thomas Gray wrote the following lines in another age which might have served as an ode to the victims of The Whitechapel murders.

> Alas, regardless of their doom
> The little victims play
> No sense have they of ills to come
> Nor care beyond today

In Memoriam
Mary Ann Nichols 1845–1888
Annie Chapman 1841–1888
Elizabeth Stride 1843–1888
Catherine Eddowes 1842–1888
Mary Jane Kelly 1863–1888

The question 'What about the victims?' has frequently been voiced in the wake of Britain's most notorious murders and especially in the aftermath of the Moors Murders which shocked the public in 1966. In the following decades, while regular attention was devoted to Myra Hindley and Ian Brady, there was little focus on their victims. Who remembers the names of the 'Brides in the Bath' or the identities of the women gassed by John Christie?

Perhaps it is the fate of murder victims to be quickly forgotten while their perpetrators achieve notoriety and fame. The names of the fallen in modern wars are rightly recorded and remembered but there are few memorials to murder victims. And, it should not be forgotten that 'victimhood', if there is such a condition, is also conferred on the families of those murdered. As the American social scientist J. L. Barkas put it in 1978, 'We are all victims'.

And, the net which ensnares victims extends even further when wrongful accusations of criminality are made or suspects are rounded up for questioning. In a sense, they too are victimised. In the case of the Ripper murders, George Hutchinson, Joseph Barnett,

Jacob Isenschmid and John Pizer were four such contemporary suspects. The mantle of being under suspicion carried its own opprobrium.

In the 125 years since Jack the Ripper's murders rocked Whitechapel and Spitalfields, scores of identities have been proposed for the otherwise anonymous murderer. Only one can possibly be correct, which means that the rest have been falsely accused and thus become unwittingly victimised in the process.

Notions of victimhood or becoming a 'murderee' have long been debated, although victimology has a more recent history. The celebrated true crime writer F. Tennyson Jesse first coined the word 'murderee' in the 1920s to describe what she called 'a race of human beings who lay themselves out to be murdered ... ', that is, individuals who are disposed to become victims.

In her book *Murder and its Motives*, Tennyson Jesse wrote that the word 'murderee' seemed to fill a 'long-held want', noting that *The Times* had adopted it. But she later wrote of wishing that she had not coined the word. At any rate, it had a short life, as 'victim' became the accepted norm.

Concepts of victimology surfaced in the late 1930s with the suggestion that the personality of the victim was a crucial factor in attracting the criminal perpetrator. And, in 1948, Hans von Hentig, a German criminologist, wrote that if there was such an individual as a 'born criminal', there must also be a 'born victim'. In his study, *The Criminal and his Victim*, he made reference to individuals who knowingly placed themselves in dangerous situations, thereby inviting sought-after excitement and, possibly, ill-treatment.

Some of this thinking was taken up in America in the mid-1950s by Marvin E. Wolfgang, Professor of Criminology at the University of Philadelphia. He conducted an analysis of over 500 murders and made a particular study of the relationship between murderers and their victims. Wolfgang set this out in his seminal work, *Patterns in Criminal Homicide*, in which he developed the concept of victim-precipitated homicide. In the dynamics between perpetrator and victim, there might be a moment when the victim initiates physical violence.

Wolfgang found from his study of Philadelphia murders that in only 14 per cent of cases were the killer and victim unknown to each other. This situation would change significantly with the advent of the serial killer, and over the next twenty years, the percentage of stranger killings in the USA rose to 30 per cent.

The interplay between murderer and victim in the Ripper killings can only be a matter of conjecture, but it was clearly a potent factor – to the extent that the perpetrator was never caught. It is commonly accepted that the Ripper's *modus operandi* was that of a serial killer. Patricia Cornwell, in her book *Portrait of a Killer*, noted that 'victims of serial murder often share some trait that is significant to the killer'. That common factor must surely be that they were prostitutes and, because of their calling, were both available and vulnerable. Joel Norris, in his book *Serial Killers*, gives a pen picture of this type of murderer whom he describes as having two effective weapons – mobility and normality. He is an individual who sees himself as a solitary stalker with a finely-tuned sense of survival.

It is tempting to think of Jack the Ripper as a lone marauder with a murderous agenda, circling the flock to target and detach a lamb for the slaughter. He knew that the East End prostitutes were easy prey for a motivated killer. But, was he really a stranger, someone from outside the area, drawn there by the availability of potential victims? Or was he an insider, a man who lived and worked in the district, totally familiar with the people and their way of life?

While a total stranger might convey a certain allure or mystery for the women he approached, he would lack the familiarity of the insider. The circumstances in which the murders were committed suggest that the perpetrator was readily accepted for his ordinariness by the women he approached, who perhaps saw him as one of their own community. Thus disarmed, they became perfect victims. This assessment seems to accord in principle with that reached by the FBI's criminal profilers in 1988.

Of the many identities and names put forward as Ripper suspects, only one can be correct, which means that the rest have become victims of circumstance and unsubstantiated allegations. This process was aided and abetted by Sir Melville Macnaghten's famous memorandum, in which he named his three suspects with the comment that he was 'inclined to exonerate the last two', thereby relegating them to the ranks of victims by association. Thus, the Macnaghten Three take their place alongside The Guildford Four and The Birmingham Six.

The third, Montague Druitt, occupies the no-man's-land between suspect and victim, with his family name placed under a permanent shadow. Long after their deaths, these suspects have been drawn into complex webs of suspicion, and as a consequence, have become victimised. One of the consequences of this game of naming and blaming is that many of the professions and organisations to which suspects belonged became tainted by association. The ripples of innuendo and suspicion spread like a viral infection.

The Metropolitan Police, and H Division in particular, were heavily criticised over their failure to catch the murderer. The public mood was famously captured in the Punch cartoon captioned 'Blind Man's Buff', which depicted a hapless, blindfolded policeman being teased by a jeering gang. Sir Charles Warren, the Police Commissioner, was already unpopular and quickly became a scapegoat. His resignation was heralded, again by Punch, with the rhyme, 'Who Killed Cock Warren?' Advice, abuse and ridicule in equal measure were heaped upon the police. Perhaps the final ignominy was Sir Arthur Conan Doyle's story, 'Jack the Harlot Killer', in which the intrepid Sherlock Holmes unmasks the Ripper, who turns out to be a police inspector.

A matrix of theorising implicating royalty, freemasonry and government produced a whirlwind of accusations. The Duke of Clarence's dalliance with a shop girl was supposed to have inspired a cover-up which involved Sir William Gull roaming around the East End in a carriage killing prostitutes to draw attention away from the scandal. But these were not just ordinary killings. They were, supposedly, carried out according to Masonic ritual echoing the Three Apprentices' killing of Hiram Abiff, builder of Solomon's Temple. The Ripper's evisceration of his victims was cited as evidence.

Suggestions that the Ripper demonstrated anatomical knowledge in the way he mutilated his victims quickly led to the idea that he was a doctor, or at least a medical student. The proximity of The London Hospital to the crime scenes led to a certain amount of harassment of medics going about their daily business. Doctors wearing dark clothing and silk hats and carrying black bags were menaced in the street by finger-pointing members of the public. The way medics dressed created the stereotypical Ripper of fiction – a truly phantasmagorical figure emerging from the mists of Whitechapel.

William Stewart's foray into Ripper studies resulted in the idea that the killer was a woman – a midwife, no less, with appropriate skills and enjoying a position of trust.

Theories that the elusive killer was a professional man became fashionable and two distinguished Victorian doctors were named as possible suspects: Sir William Gull and Sir John Williams. Added to these were Doctors Tumblety and Donston Stephenson.

It would be natural perhaps to think that known murderers might have extended their range and included the Whitechapel murders in their portfolio. Dr Neill Cream, who allegedly hinted at his credentials while on the scaffold, and George Chapman, fell into this category. And, ironically, James Maybrick, putative author of The Ripper's Diary, suffered a loss of grace by being poisoned by his wife – a case of the perpetrator made victim!

One group of unsuspecting victims were members of the creative and artistic communities who became targets for suspicion. Walter Sickert, for example, was known for selecting subjects of morbid interest for his paintings. And Richard Mansfield, the American actor, succeeded in frightening audiences at the Lyceum Theatre with his performance in Dr Jekyll and Mr Hyde which involved a dramatic transformation from gentle soul to devil incarnate. Such was the impact he made on stage, that many thought he was the Ripper in real life. Unusual interests and eccentricity provided shortcuts to suspicions and accusations. Necromancers and practitioners of the Black Arts fell into this category. Few claimed self-knowledge of murderous acts but others, such as Aleister Crowley, had it claimed on their behalf.

Minority groups were also subjected to finger-pointing, particularly the Irish and Jewish populations who were settled in various East End parishes. Irish immigrants formed a sizeable proportion of the very poor and attracted resentful comments, but accusatory remarks were particularly directed to people of Jewish origin. The conviction of Israel Lipski in 1887 did the Jewish community no favours and

'Lipski' was used in the streets as a pejorative term. Matters were not helped by George Hutchinson's reference to the Jewishness of the man he claimed to have seen in the company of Mary Kelly. Added to this was Sir Robert Anderson's insistence that the Ripper was a 'Polish Jew'.

These and other aspects of victimhood are dealt with at length by the contributors to this book. The authors are veteran Ripper chroniclers, familiar with the highways and byways of the Ripper road map. They share the principle that in all the plethora of commentaries about the Whitechapel Murderer, there are many categories of victim apart from the five women slain in the streets in the autumn of 1888. Numerous individuals and organisations were touched by the tentacles of suspicion and accusation and, as part of the process, we all become victims, if only by allowing ourselves to be led down false trails.

Thomas Gray's verse is taken from his poem, *Ode on a Distant Prospect of Eton College*. Angels of Sorrow is the title of a CD produced by Frogg Moody and Ian Marshall in 2002, honouring the memory of the victims of the Whitechapel Murderer. Proceeds from sales were donated to Victim Support Tower Hamlets.

The
Whitechapel Society
1888

By Frogg Moody

Following on from the success of our first publication for The History Press, *Jack the Ripper – The Suspects*, The Whitechapel Society is delighted to present this new offering, *Jack the Ripper – The Terrible Legacy*. Once again we have brought together ten researchers and authors from within our ranks to produce a second volume of notable 'others' who were, or have become, victims as a direct result of the Whitechapel murders.

The Freemasons, the Royal Family, Government officials, Police officials, Suspects – these are just some of the unfortunate victims who became embroiled in the events of that Autumn of Terror of 1888.

It seems fitting that the Whitechapel Society should be asked to compile this new book on Jack the Ripper and victimology, because our organisation has become the largest and most successful society in the world dedicated to studying the subject. The Whitechapel Society has grown in leaps and bounds since Mark Galloway had the brilliant idea to create it in 1995, and recent events have included our largest and most successful ever Jack the Ripper UK conference.

Our revamped website, Facebook and YouTube groups, membership meetings in London's East End and our critically acclaimed magazine *The Whitechapel Journal* have helped us increase our range and presence. However, our enthusiasm for researching and studying the Victorian world of Jack the Ripper has remained unchanged since the early days and we feel sure the pages of this new volume will illustrate this.

If you would like to become a member of the Whitechapel Society and enjoy the immense benefits of being closely associated with a community of historical experts, enthusiasts and aficionados, please go to our website at: www.whitechapelsociety.com

In recent years The Whitechapel Society has diversified, broadened its horizons and explored new, exciting ways of bringing the past to life. Members have been encouraged to participate in a whole host of events including a Photographic History of London's Old East End, short story competitions, public exhibitions and *Question Time* debates. The Whitechapel Society is also proud to be on the steering group of the Tower Hamlets Historical Archives at The Bancroft Library.

ONE

'There is More Than One Way to Lose Your Life to a Killer'

The Screen Depiction of Inspector Abberline

By Clare Smith

'There is more than one way to lose your life to a killer' is the tagline from the 2007 film *Zodiac*. The film tells the story of the Zodiac Killer, arguably the world's most infamous unidentified serial killer after Jack the Ripper. The film traces how the lives of the people investigating the crimes are destroyed by their search for the killer, even though they are not victims of violence. In the same way as the on-screen inspector suffers in his search for the Zodiac Killer, Frederick Abberline is a victim of Jack the Ripper; his posthumous reputation has been destroyed. He is shown as suffering from drug or alcohol addiction, attempted murder and colluding with the conspiracy to protect the identity of the culprit.

Inspector Abberline, along with all of the police involved in the investigation of Jack the Ripper, were victims in that they failed to catch the killer. Indeed there is a negativity that is used to depict the police in general in films about Jack the Ripper, and I would suggest that this is based on the negative attitudes of the late nineteenth century public towards the police.

The public perception of the police force in 1888 was not favourable; it may be argued that the police's fall from grace in the public consciousness occurred in 1860 with the investigation of the murder of Francis Saville Kent by Jack Whicher. In her examination of the case, Kate Summerscale writes that before the case police detectives were perceived as 'figures of mystery and glamour, the surreptitious, all seeing gods of London.'

However after Whicher had literally aired the family's dirty laundry and brought charges against one of the daughters of the house, this perception shifted and the detective became 'a shadowy figure, a demon as well as a demi god.' This unfavourable perception was further developed by the Contagious Diseases Act legislation, repealed in 1886, which allowed the police to accuse a woman of prostitution on sight, at least one woman committed suicide as result of such a false accusation.

In 1887, the year before the Ripper murders, two more events further damned the police in the eyes of the public. Firstly the publication of W. T. Stead's series of articles entitled 'The Maiden Tribute of Modern Babylon', which campaigned against child prostitution. In these articles the police came across as uncaring and ineffective, joking with Stead that if they ran into every home where screaming was heard, they would attend more childbirths than doctors. For the working classes, the death knell for the police's reputation as heroes came with the police response to the Bloody Sunday demonstration of 1887. The police, especially Sir Charles Warren, were viewed as having overreacted to the presence of protestors in Trafalgar Square. This view was still held during the Whitechapel murders; in a letter to *The Daily Telegraph* from 19 September the police were said to have 'by a series of blunders, angered the mob in Trafalgar Square and made it dangerous.'

During the murders the press was critical of the police investigation. *Punch* ran a cartoon of a policeman wearing a blindfold and being pushed around by the criminal classes. The letters pages of the newspapers were full of advice for the police, from the practical letters recommending the beat police be issued with rubber-soled boots so that they could patrol the streets silently to the suggestion that recruitment of policemen be 'selected more for their brain power and ability to meet cunning with cunning, than for their height and chest measurements.' The idea that can be gathered from the newspapers is that the police were heavy-footed idiots blundering around Whitechapel.

In films about the Ripper, the upper ranks of the police are shown as not caring about the murders and having no respect for the victims. In the television series *Jack The Ripper*, Florrie – an East End prostitute – can identify the Ripper, so Charles Warren uses her as bait to catch the killer, as a 'prostitute place[s] no value on herself, so why should we?' The uniformed police are also shown as bumbling and idiotic in *What the Swedish Butler Saw*. In this film, the police search a house for the Ripper, yet fail to realise that a figure hiding behind the aspidistra is actually a woman. The policeman congratulates the owner on such a fine specimen (the plant) – shame about the sculpture! Hardly the astute observation of Sherlock Holmes!

Of all the police who investigated the murders, it is Inspector Abberline who is given the most screen time, and his presentation has more depth and thought. While the upper ranks of the police are callous and the lower ranks bumbling, Abberline is depicted as genuinely caring about the victims, with a determination to catch the killer. Yet Abberline is still presented in a negative fashion on-screen and his life transformed into fiction; I believe this loss of identity makes him a victim of the Ripper.

The 22 September 1888 publication of Punch criticised the police during the investigation with the drawing 'Blind-Man's Buff' – 'Turn around three times, and catch whom you may!'

Before looking at how Abberline is transformed into a fictional character, it is necessary to present the facts of his life. Frederick Abberline was born in Dorset in 1843, and worked as a clocksmith until 1863. During his police service, Abberline worked in Whitechapel from 1873 until 1887, and was so well-thought-of in the area that he was presented with a watch by the residents when he left, as a mark of respect. In 1888 Abberline was a married man; he had married his second wife in 1876 and they were together until his death in 1929. In his spare time Abberline enjoyed gardening, and after he left the police force he worked for Pinkerton's Detective Agency, policing the Gaming Rooms in Monte Carlo before retiring to Bournemouth.

The consensus amongst those who research the Whitechapel murders is that Abberline could not have done more to catch Jack, and risked his health in the time he devoted to the case. In an interview with the *Pall Mall Gazette* in 1903 Abberline described how he would often walk the streets in the early morning and had ' … given those wretched and homeless women, who were Jack the Ripper's special prey, four pence or sixpence for shelter to get them away from the streets and out of harm's way.' He also never lost his desire to see the Ripper caught, following murder cases with interest and contacting the *Pall Mall Gazette* when George Chapman was arrested to state his belief that the Ripper was finally arrested.

This dedicated, married, West Country gardener is not the Abberline that we see on-screen. The two most in-depth presentations of Abberline on-screen are found in *Jack the Ripper* and *From Hell*. While both of these productions are based on the same primary source – the Whitechapel murders – the secondary sources for the narratives differ and this affects the portrayal of Abberline.

The opening credits of *Jack the Ripper* inform the viewer that it is the result of official documentation from the Home Office and Scotland Yard, which suggests to the viewer that they are watching a docudrama. However, as will become apparent in the analysis of this presentation of Abberline, more than a little artistic licence is taken with facts.

From Hell is based upon the graphic novel by Alan Moore and Eddie Campbell, which is in turn influenced by Stephen Knight's *Jack the Ripper: the Final Solution*. In the appendix to *From Hell*, Moore writes of the meeting between William Gull and John Merrick ('The Elephant Man') that it is

Inspector Frederick George Abberline (Toby, 7 January 1888). Abberline has been presented in a negative fashion on screen.

'fictional, although plausible'. This means that both the graphic novel and the film have a freer approach to facts and biography.

While both depictions differ in origins, they share some common elements. Both present Abberline as a working-class cockney, local to Whitechapel. In *Jack the Ripper*, when challenged by the leader of the Whitechapel Vigilante Group that he does not care about the victims, Abberline responds that he grew up with these people. His connection to the people of Whitechapel is also shown via his knowing the name of a young pickpocket and having an informer from the area.

In *From Hell*, Abberline has a strong cockney accent and understands the economy of Whitechapel. When Charles Warren fails to grasp the importance of the grape stalk found underneath the body of Polly Nichols, Abberline explains that no one in Whitechapel could afford grapes, therefore the killer must be able to afford them.

The reason for changing Abberline's socio-economic background, I would argue, lies in the presentation of the upper ranks of the police and the screen Ripper, both of whom are depicted as upper class. By depicting Abberline – the hero of the film who is dedicated to catching the killer – as closer to the class and local identity of the victims, it is another way of positioning Abberline in opposition to the killer. It is an interesting narrative device but does erode Abberline's identity, his class altered to support the class of the Ripper which is a form of victimisation.

The second similarity in the depiction of Abberline in *From Hell* and *Jack the Ripper* is addiction; in the former Abberline is addicted to drugs, and in the latter he is an alcoholic. Neither of these have any basis in fact; indeed at the 2011 Whitechapel Society conference, the writer and director of *Jack the Ripper* (David Wickes) denied that Abberline was portrayed as an alcoholic. Wickes argued that Abberline was simply depicted as a man who liked a drink, but I read the film in a different way, and I would propose that the majority of the audience would do the same and view Abberline as an alcoholic. The first time the audience see Abberline, he is sleeping in a cell with empty whisky bottles on the floor. During the film, Abberline's partner Sergeant Godley 'polices' Abberline's sobriety in the same way that Dr Watson polices Holmes' addiction in the *Sherlock Holmes* canon.

In *From Hell* Abberline is addicted to drugs; he is seen smoking an opium pipe and adding laudanum to absinthe. Again, Sergeant Godley attempts to manage the addiction, searching for Abberline in opium dens when the case begins and warning uniformed policemen not to mention where Abberline was found. In the graphic novel *From Hell* Abberline is not a drug addict; nor do any of the sources on Abberline's life mention any drug addiction. The film version of *From Hell* did not initially have Abberline using drugs. This was an addition added by the casting of Johnny Depp as Abberline. In an online article on the making of *From Hell* it was noted that 'as the film progressed, the Hughes Brothers added a few opium-smoking additions to Depp's character. Just the kind of tics that appeal to Johnny. 'I liked the idea that he was this very good inspector,' Depp says, 'but he had his dark side – that he was a bit of a junkie really.' The audience would be aware that Depp has used drugs and discussed his experiences in the media; this would inform his reading of Abberline and his performance.

One of the ways that victims of serial killers are further victimised is that they become 'public property': their lives analysed and changed on-screen, or in literature to suit the narrative that the writer or actor desires. In *From Hell* Abberline suffers the same fate; his behaviour and reputation is damaged, because like the physical victims of a killer, he has become public property, open to interpretation. The result of this interpretation is Abberline's depiction in *The Wolfman*. To add to the film's presentation as 'Victorian Gothic', Abberline is cast as the detective investigating the mysterious happenings on the moors. This is clearly after 1888, as he is asked if he had been involved in 'that Whitechapel business'. Abberline again fails to stop the killer, in this instance a werewolf. After the final confrontation with the werewolf, Abberline is bitten, and at the next full moon will become a monster. Abberline can now be added to fiction and made into a killer.

Once it had been decided to incorporate drug use into Abberline's character in *From Hell*, it becomes a motif to link Abberline to Jack the Ripper. The ritual of Abberline preparing the absinthe and laudanum cocktail while listening to a gramophone is visually juxtaposed with the ritual of the Ripper dressing to go out and kill while listening to the gramophone. There is a trend in detective fiction for the detective to have more in common with the killer than other members of society. An example of this is Thomas Harris' novel *Red Dragon*, where Will Graham is mentally and physically scarred by his ability to relate to serial killers.

By depicting Abberline with a vice such as drug or alcohol addiction, the character becomes more familiar to an audience used to watching flawed detectives. Both *Jack the Ripper* and *From Hell* go one step further in linking Abberline and Jack; they show Abberline attempting to take the law into his own hands and use violence by shooting William Gull when he is revealed as the Ripper. In both films Abberline is prevented from committing murder, but is shown as being willing to kill and not arrest the Ripper.

In establishing a connection between Abberline and the Ripper in terms of indulging in taboo behaviour and a tendency towards violence, the films clearly highlight the similarities between detective and killer. However, this narrative device sacrifices the reputation of Abberline, and changes him from a man who did all he could to catch Jack the Ripper to a man who had to be sobered up to investigate the case.

The screen Abberline is unmarried; in *Jack the Ripper* he is single and in *From Hell* he is a widower. At the time of the murders Abberline was actually married, but this part of his biography is changed for narrative purposes. In *Jack the Ripper* it allows him to have a failed relationship that he is trying to rekindle, and in *From Hell* he becomes romantically involved with Mary Kelly. In *Jack the Ripper*, the investigation into the Whitechapel murders causes Abberline's attempts at reconciliation to fail. This places him in the detective genre of divorced, heavy-drinking male detectives that the audience is familiar with from films and literature.

In *From Hell*, Abberline's relationship with Mary Kelly fails, but in more positive way. Abberline sacrifices his chance of happiness with Mary to ensure her safety; an act reminiscent of Rick from *Casablanca*, staying behind to allow the woman he loves to live a better life. The negative side of this portrayal is that this loss causes Abberline's death: at the end of the film he is found dead in an opium den, with two coins in his hand to pay Charon to cross into the underworld. Abberline's suicide is due to the fact that he has had to collude with the conspiracy and is unable to be with the woman he loves. In reality Abberline retired to Bournemouth and died of old age; a much more genteel ending than suicide in an opium den.

At the end of *Jack the Ripper*, the credits give details of what happened to those involved in the Whitechapel murders. In Abberline's case, the audience is told that he left the police after the Cleveland Street scandal. An interesting choice of words, that: not the Cleveland Street investigation, but scandal. This implies that Abberline was a 'dirty cop'; that not only did Abberline collude with the conspiracy that protected William Gull, but that he was involved in a second cover-up for the aristocracy. This is an assertion made by Stephen Knight, and picked up by *Jack the Ripper* and *From Hell*, that while Abberline did not instigate the conspiracy to protect the Ripper, he did go along with it.

Audiences believe what they are shown on film. The lack of legal protection available for those depicted on film often leads to victimisation. The family of Agatha Christie sued the makers of the film *Agatha*, which depicted a fictionalised version of the eleven days Christie went missing in 1926. The judge rejected the suit on the grounds that 'where a fictionalized account of an event in the life of a public figure is depicted in a novel or movie, it is evident to the public that the events depicted are fictitious.' I would challenge this in the case of Abberline, for both *Jack the Ripper* and *From Hell* achieve historic authenticity in set design and costume; they aim to convince an audience that they are watching the depiction of real events.

Were it not for his involvement in the Whitechapel murders investigation, Abberline would never have been depicted as an alcoholic or drug addict, bad policeman, willing to use violence rather than the law, or had his biography so drastically altered. Abberline never sought to become a public figure, yet because of the crimes of Jack the Ripper he has become a semi-fictionalised character, open to interpretation. In this way, film has made Inspector Abberline a victim of Jack the Ripper.

Bibliography

Films

Agatha, Michael Apted, dir. (Sweetwall,1979)
A Man with a Maid, or What the Swedish Butler Saw, Vernon P. Becker, dir. (Unicorn Enterprises, 1975)
Casblanca, Michael Curtiz, dir. (Warner Bros. 1942)
Jack The Ripper, David Wickes, dir. (various, 1988)
The Wolfman, Joe Johnston, dir. (Universal Pictures, 2010)
Zodiac, David Fincher, dir. (Paramount Pictures, 2007)

Books

Aquino, John T., *Truth and Lives on Film: The Legal Problems of Depicting Real Persons and Events in a Fictional Medium* (Jefferson, McFarland & Co., 2005)
Moore, Alan, and Campbell, Eddie, *From Hell* (Knockabout Comics, 2002)
Ryder, Stephen P. (ed), *Public Reactions to Jack the Ripper: Letters to the Editor August-December 1888* (Inklings Press, 2006)
Summerscale, Kate, *The Suspicions of Mr Whicher or The Murder at Road Mill House* (London, Bloomsbury, 2008)

Other

Pall Mall Gazette 24 March 1903
www.interviewjohnnydepp-zone2.com accessed on 12 June 2012

Clare Smith

Clare Smith works for the National Museum of Wales as Collection Manager for the Art collection. She is researching a PhD examining Jack the Ripper on film, and has a MA Honours degree in History of Art, a MA in Mythology and Society. Her research interests are narrative structure and iconography.

TWO

Jack The Ripper – a Freemason?

The Victims of Accusations

by Yasha Beresiner

It is gratifying to participate in the wide outlook given by the title of this book and include genuine victims beyond the sad and miserable deaths of the now infamous East End prostitutes. Every suspect hounded by the police, publicised by the press and admonished by the public was a victim, to some extent. Certainly the Jewish community in the area had its fair share of victimisation, aspects of which are included in this book. In this context, the accusations and theories of the involvement of the Freemasons in Jack the Ripper murders were the most extraordinary, and strangely accepted by a wide and international circle. It should not be surprising, maybe, to find a credulous audience for a society at the time seen as secretive and powerful. An anti-Masonic culture was prevalent, just as an anti-Semitic one was, and a well-told story of intrigue and mischief was easily accepted by the general public. Interestingly, in all the available literature on the subject, there has never been a direct connection made between the Jews and Freemasons as perpetrators of the murders, though both have been separately accused of the crimes. This is in spite of the fact that, particularly among the uninitiated, Freemasonry is closely equated with Judaism. The reason is because the Masonic legends frequently emphasise the craft's close connections with King Solomon's Temple.

Here is an opportunity, therefore, to clear the air of mystery that surrounds Freemasonry and demolish any suspicions left that the Freemasons were in any way involved in the Whitechapel murders.

Walter Sickert

The Jack the Ripper Masonic conspiracy theory begins with the famous painter and etcher, Walter Sickert (1860–1942) who was not a Freemason. Sickert was born in Munich and arrived in London at the age of eight. In 1911 he founded 'The Camden Town Group' of artists, enlarged and renamed three years later as the well-known 'London Group'. He is regarded by some as the greatest British painter after Turner, before the advent of Francis Bacon. Sickert was implicated (not for the first time) in the Jack the Ripper murders when Patricia Cornwell's *Portrait of a Killer: Jack the Ripper – Case Closed* was published in 2003 and placed him on the list of 'definite' suspects. She made much of his violent, psychopathic mind and came up with supposed clear-cut DNA and other evidence of his intimate knowledge of the murders, proven by his art. She claimed visual evidence of a direct, confessional link in Sickert's paintings to the Whitechapel murders. It is true that Sickert painted naked prostitutes, in a state of sleep or who appeared on the verge of death. In one of his paintings called 'Camden Town Murder', we see a naked prostitute on a bed with a fully-clothed man sitting by her side. Most of Cornwell's theories, however, have been discredited and dismissed, and to follow this any further would extend beyond the scope of this chapter.

The relevant point is that Sickert had already been linked to the Whitechapel murders by Stephen Knight almost thirty years earlier, as an unwilling accomplice in a Masonic conspiracy to cover up for the Duke of Clarence, which is where our story begins.

The Camden Town Murder painting by Walter Sickert.

'Eddy' the Duke of Clarence

Albert Victor, Duke of Clarence, known to his family as 'Eddy', was Queen Victoria's dissolute grandson. His father, who later became King Edward VII, was Grand Master of the United Grand Lodge of England in 1888. Unfortunately, Eddy's passion for unsavoury activities in the East End of London finally led him to suffer from syphilis which affected his brain, and he died at the young age of twenty-eight. The Royal connection arose because both his mother and grandmother (Princess Alexandra and Queen Victoria respectively) wanted to educate the rather insular Prince and encouraged him to visit Walter Sickert to expand his artistic education. It was here, at Walter Sickert's studio in Cleveland Street in Camden, that Eddy first met, fell in love and finally secretly married Annie Elizabeth Crook, an illiterate Catholic girl, who worked in the bakery across the road. They had a child named Alice Margaret Crook. The nanny for the baby was purported to be the unfortunate Mary Kelly, who, in the company of Walter Sickert, was a witness to their wedding.

Knight's Masonic conspiracy theory, implicating royalty and the government, was that the only solution to prevent the public outcry and dramatic consequences that might follow discovery was to bring in the Freemasons. They would act according to Masonic ritual and silence the witnesses to the union. These witnesses happened to be five wretched women who had to resort to prostitution to make a living and survive: thus the theory of the five 'Masonic' assassinations.

The Conspiracy Theory

The origins of the Masonic conspiracy theory go back to the November 1970 edition of *The Criminologist* which carried an article by a Dr Thomas Stowell. Here, thinly-disguised accusations were made ('the murders were committed by "S", the heir to power and wealth'). The interpretation was that Prince Albert, the future heir to the throne, was Jack the Ripper!

These accusations were compounded in a BBC drama documentary that followed in 1973, titled *Jack the Ripper*. Stephen Knight had worked as a researcher for the BBC for this programme, and he decided to pursue the story further. He came across a certain Joseph Gorman, who called himself Joseph Sickert, and who claimed that the heretofore childless artist Walter Sickert was his father. Furthermore, according to Joseph, shortly before his death in 1942, the artist had confessed to his part in the murders. The story – as now reported by Stephen Knight – was that the Freemasons, with the knowledge of members of the Royal Family (who were themselves Freemasons) were involved in a murderous cover up of the Prince's clandestine marriage to Annie Crook. The Prime Minister himself, Lord Salisbury, had been instructed by Queen Victoria personally to resolve the matter discreetly

T. E. A. STOWELL, C.B.E., M.D., F.R.C.S.

Mr. T. E. A. Stowell, formerly honorary surgeon, Victoria Infirmary, Northwich, and consulting surgeon in the Emergency Medical Service, died on 8 November at his home in Southampton at the age of 80.

Thomas Edmund Alexander Stowell was born on 1 January 1890 and was educated at St. Paul's School, and St. Thomas's Hospital, where he was Tite scholar, qualifying with the Conjoint diploma in 1910.  He held early appointments at St. Thomas's Hospital, Grimsby and District Hospital, and the Royal Southern Hospital, Liverpool. In 1912 he took the F.R.C.S. and became assistant ophthalmic surgeon at St. Andrew's Hospital, Bromley-by-Bow, and Battersea General Hospital, and surgeon at

national Council of Industrial Health held in London in 1948 he worked very hard to make it the great success it proved to be, and in recognition of his services was appointed C.B.E. in the following year. He was also chairman of the British Committee of International Congresses on Industrial Health and Safety, and a member of various other medical societies and institutions both at home and abroad.

He was interested in criminology, and in an article published in *The Criminologist* said that for fifty years he had kept to himself certain evidence as to the identity of the notorious killer Jack the Ripper, which seemed to point to a man of noble family, for fear of involving as witnesses some close friends who were still alive.

He married in 1913 Lilian Elizabeth Wagner, who survives him together with their son. Their only daughter died in an accident in 1958.

D.H. writes: I first met Tom Stowell in 1946, when he presided at the first meeting of the British organizing council for the Ninth International Congress

The obituary of Dr Thomas Stowell. His article in the 1970 edition of The Criminologist caused a sensation.

and without fuss. Accordingly, the Masons, members of Salisbury's own Masonic Lodge, were to be the agents of the Crown and State, selected to 'eliminate' all those who knew the truth: that a child had resulted from the Duke's illicit union with the wretched Annie. A fact that – if discovered by the public at this delicate time – could topple the very monarchy of the United Kingdom.

This Royal–Masonic conspiracy theory reached its zenith with the 1976 publication of Stephen Knight's sensational book *Jack the Ripper: The Final Solution*. The one and only source for Knight's theory and 300-page book was Joseph Sickert, self-proclaimed illegitimate son of Walter Sickert. If Joseph Sickert is eliminated from the equation there is no Masonic conspiracy, and in fact, Joseph Sickert later retracted his 'evidence' and publicly admitted it had been a hoax.

The interest generated by Knight's book led to a flurry of films and publications in the following decades: in 1979 the movie *Murder by Decree* first appeared, still being shown on television to this day. It was followed by a book by Melvyn Fairclough titled *The Ripper and the Royals* in 1991, and *From Hell* which made its first appearance in 1999. The authors, Alan Moore and Eddie Campbell, referred to their work as a 'graphic novel', but it has been reviewed as a 'well-researched comic book'. In 2001 the now famous movie was released under the same name, directed by Albert Hughes and starring Johnny Depp as Inspector Frederick Abberline.

Popularity of Freemasonry

At the time of the Whitechapel murders there were over 120 potential suspects. None of these contemporary suspects are recorded as being Freemasons, despite the fact that Freemasonry was at the height of its popularity at the time. The Prince of Wales, later King Edward VII, had been appointed Grand Master in 1874 and he brought Freemasonry into fashion. It continued to the end of the century and beyond.

The origins of Freemasonry remain somewhat vague until the formation of the fraternity as an organised body in 1717. The success of Freemasonry, compared to the many similar contemporary organisations, was reliant on its ability to attract the patronage of the nobility and aristocracy and, by 1747, royalty itself. Today the society continues in the long tradition of having royalty at its head. The current Grand Master is Prince Edward, Duke of Kent; a grandson of George V and first cousin to Queen Elizabeth II.

Operative Stonemasons

Like the origins, the source of the unique Masonic ceremonies in the various proceedings is also a matter of conjecture. What is certain is that today's Freemasons emulate the long-standing traditions of the working stonemasons of medieval times. They replicate practices, symbols and ceremonies of ancient operative Masons. There are no unique, original symbols or rituals in modern Freemasonry. They have all been adopted from elsewhere. Every square and compass, trowel and plumb rule, obligation and prayer, has originated with some other body or organisation, often the medieval stonemasons themselves, and can be viewed in an historic context. There is, however, no evidence that the modern Mason is a direct descendant of these stonemasons. Thus the rituals and penalties, at times seen by the uninitiated as sinister, are no more than a display of traditions that may at one time have been relevant to the working members of an active guild. They play no part in current Freemasonry, other than in a symbolic and traditional content. They may be seen as membership-galvanising theatrical enactments.

Masonic Penalties

These symbolic penalties – which Stephen Knight was to criticise and dramatise in his later book *The Brotherhood* – were referred to in order explain why and how the Freemasons were involved in the Whitechapel murders. What Knight ignored

A Masonic penalty being implemented.

was the practical traditions of the medieval guild system of the operative masons, practical traditions that have no place in modern Freemasonry (the words 'guild' and 'company' are interchangeable). These traditions have been symbolically adopted by modern Freemasons. The working stonemasons of long ago – members of the London Company of Masons with records dating to the fourteenth century – belonged to an exclusive, lifelong and protective union: their guild. Membership, as was the case with all Livery Companies, ('livery' referring to the distinguishing attire they were allowed to wear) was a closed shop. The skills and knowledge acquired over many years of apprenticeship and experience were keenly protected. To reveal any of these secrets to an outsider would weaken the guild. It could potentially allow an outsider to benefit from privileges normally available only to members. This was tantamount to stealing the livelihood of a brother Mason. It was severely punishable with expulsion, which was as good a threat as death, since a worker could not be employed unless he belonged to a guild. The guild not only provided work, but also protected the mason and his family for life. It even provided burial after death. After his demise, the Livery Company would ensure proper funeral rites, so essential in medieval England to assure a heavenly afterlife. The Company would care for the deceased member's widow until her death, and ensure the education of his children. In return, total obedience and commitment and secrecy of the art and 'mystery' of the trade were required. In modern times, the rhetoric has remained the same; the actions, however, are symbolic and historic only.

Ripper Victims

The Whitechapel series of murders, which took place during the space of just seven weeks, had five 'canonical' victims: Mary Ann ('Polly') Nichols murdered on 31 August 1888; Annie Chapman on 8 September 1888; Elizabeth Stride and Catherine Eddowes on 30 September 1888 and Mary Jane Kelly on 9 November 1888. All these women had been engaged in prostitution. This fact, more than any other, seems to have been the cause for their demise at the hands of a violent sexual serial killer. All of them had their throats cut across, four from 'ear to ear', the cause of their death, after which their bodies were brutally mutilated. The 'evidence' of Masonic involvement, according to Knight, is apparent in the Masonic penalties that were reflected in the injuries inflicted on the victims, in addition to the cutting of the throat. According to Stephen Knight, the Ripper murders are strewn with these Masonic references. He gives a plethora of evidence: Annie Chapman's tongue protruded between her teeth and was swollen (the tongue symbolising silence, being part of Masonic ritual); Mary Kelly's heart had been removed; Annie Chapman and Catherine Eddowes had their abdomens cut open and intestines removed. In addition, Catherine Eddowes had severe cuts on her face in the shape of inverted triangles. Stephen Knight claims that the triangles have a precise Masonic relevance. Eddowes' body was found in Mitre Square, a site expressly selected by the Masons, according to Knight, because here once stood the altar of an ancient monastic abbey riddled with Masonic connections. Furthermore, according to Knight, the mitre and the square are basic tools of the Freemason. The fanciful list of similar examples is unending.

Charles Warren

One person pivotal to Knight's Masonic conspiracy theory was the head of the Metropolitan Police Force at the time, Commissioner Sir Charles Warren, who resigned his post on 9 November 1888 – the day of the last Jack the Ripper murder. An ex-soldier with a regimental tradition, and a high-ranking Freemason (he was also the first Master of my own *Quatuor Coronati* Lodge in London in 1886), he is accused by Knight of a cover-up of evidence of the Freemasons' involvement in the sordid murders. The Goulston Street graffito may be the biggest 'red herring ' in the Masonic conspiracy theory. Charles Warren was called to the scene before dawn on the morning following the double murder on 30 September 1888. A constable had discovered an inscription written in chalk on the inside wall of No 8 Goulston Street. The five line inscription read:

> The Juwes are
> The men That
> Will not
> be Blamed
> for nothing

Without hesitation, and fearing anti-Semitic reprisals, Warren ordered the officer present to wipe out the inscription before the light of day would reveal it to a volatile and excited public. This action, according to Knight, was clear-cut evidence that the writing was of Masonic consequence. The word 'Juwes' in particular, was of important significance to Masons and indicated the involvement of the fraternity. The writing had to be deleted to avoid the discovery of the conspirators. Furthermore, the only tangible artefact surviving from the murders was part of Catherine Eddowes' apron on which the killer had wiped his knife, found nearby. Further definite evidence, according to Knight, of the involvement of Freemasons, who wear aprons in their ceremonies! (I cannot, finally, avoid the use of an exclamation mark).

Sequel

The sequel to these events is that Walter Sickert eventually became Alice Crook's lover. She gave birth to the Joseph Sickert who, as has been repeatedly stated, was the sole source for Stephen Knight's intriguing and unsupported outrageous theory. But of greater consequence, Joseph Gorman, aka Joseph Sickert, in an interview with The Sunday Times of London in June 1978 stated that the whole of his story '... was a hoax; I made it all up', he said. He described it as 'a whopping fib' and pure invention. Stephen Knight dismissed Sickert's denial as unintentional, and induced by fear and embarrassment.

The truth is that blatant weaknesses appeared in Stephen Knight's book the moment it was published. It was a repeated and now enhanced theory, soon to be proven false and ridiculous. There were too many inaccuracies for the book to be given any credence. It has rightly now been dismissed as total nonsense, albeit making fascinating fictitious reading.

Thus, back to the original question: Was Jack the Ripper a Freemason? The answer must be: He might have been ... he might also have been an odd fellow or a golfer! You are free to decide.

Bibliography

Articles

Stowell, Dr Thomas, 'Jack the Ripper – A Solution?' *The Criminologist* (November 1970)

Books

Cornwell, Patricia, *Portrait of a Killer: Jack the Ripper – Case Closed* (Berkeley,2003)
Fairclough, Mervyn, *The Ripper & The Royals* (Duckworth, 1991)
Knight, Stephen, *Jack the Ripper: The Final Solution* (George G. Harrap & Co. Ltd, 1976)
Knight, Stephen, *The Brotherhood* (Granada Publishing, 1984)
Moore, Alan, and Campbell, Eddie, *From Hell* (Knockabout Comics, 1999)

Films

Jack the Ripper (BBC, 1973)
Murder by Decree, Bob Clark, dir. (Canadian Film Development Corporation, 1979)
From Hell, Hughes, Albert, and Hughes, Allan, dir. (Twentieth Century Fox, 2001)

Yasha Beresiner

Yasha Beresiner was born in Istanbul, received his law degree from the Hebrew University in Jerusalem, and settled in England in 1963. Following a legal career he converted his hobbies into a business, with a shop, 'InterCol London', in the Camden Passage London. He is a city guide, past Master of a Livery Company, a senior Freemason and a prolific author. His website: www.intercol.co.uk

THREE

The Victims of George Chapman

By Sue Parry

Severin Klosowski, aka George Chapman, is the most likely candidate for Jack the Ripper.[1]

He was born Severin Antonio Klosowski in Poland in 1865 and arrived in the UK in early 1888. Initially he worked as a barber, but became a licensed victualler in 1897. He changed his name to George Chapman in about 1893.

Chapman was hanged for the murder of Maud Marsh in 1902; however, there is no doubt that he was also responsible for the deaths of Mary Isabella Spink in 1897 and Bessie Taylor in 1901. All three women died as a result of arsenic and/or antimony poisoning. If Chapman was the Whitechapel murderer of 1888, then these three women are victims of Jack the Ripper. However, they were not his only victims; their families and friends and even Chapman's own wife and daughter all suffered at his hand.

Chapman's first murder victim was Mary Isabella Spink. She was born Mary Isabella Renton in 1858 and had already suffered a tragic life before she met Chapman. Mary was the first child of William Renton, a linen draper, and his wife Ann Eliza Renton (*née* Smith). Mary was born in Pudsey, now a suburb of Leeds. However, tragedy was to strike when Mary lost her baby brother George in 1867, her mother in April 1868, and her father in January 1869. Mary and her sister Clara were left orphans. Mary was ten and Clara eight.

Mary's maternal aunt Sarah Ann Smith had married Mary's father's brother Alfred Renton, and if things were not tragic enough, Mary's Uncle Alfred died in 1865 aged just twenty-seven, leaving a wife and three children. Mary's maternal grandmother took her widowed daughter with her three children plus her two orphaned grandchildren into her home. However, this does not appear to have been an impoverished family, as the 1871 census shows that along with the two women and five children, there were also two servants living in the household. It was also revealed at Chapman's trial many years later that Mary had inherited £600 from her grandfather. As Mary reached adulthood, she left the care of her grandmother and followed her cousin Joseph (one of Sarah's children) to Leytonstone.

It was there that Mary met and married Shadrach Spink in December 1883. Their first child, Shadrach, was born in April the following year. In early 1889 Mary gave birth to a second son, William Alfred. William was destined to be another of Chapman's victims. Joseph was to later testify at Chapman's trial that Shadrach left Mary a few months before she gave birth to William, taking young Shadrach with him. The 1891 census shows Mary living alone 'by her own means' (presumably her inheritance), with her son William in Leyton. Meanwhile William's father and brother were living with his paternal grandparents in Norfolk.

George Chapman was born Severin Antonio Klosowski in Poland in 1865 and arrived in the UK in early 1888.

We can only speculate about the cause of this marital breakdown, but for a man to leave his wife and take just one of his children with him, leaving the other with its mother, suggests that maybe Shadrach suspected Mary of infidelity and believed that the second child was not his. Shadrach was named as the baby's father on the birth certificate, though the informant was Mary. As a married woman may register her husband as being the father of her baby without the husband being present at the registration, it is possible that Shadrach was unaware that he was named as the baby's father. Shadrach's doubts would appear to be confirmed by the fact that even after Mary's death, Shadrach and baby William were never reunited. So by the age of two, the only person in William's world was his mother Mary.

However, when William was six, his mother met Chapman and it was not long before Mary and young William were lodging in the same house where Chapman had a furnished room in Forest Road, Leyton. Chapman recorded in his diary that he and Mary were married on 27 October. However, there was no marriage, but to the outside world Chapman and Mary presented themselves as a married couple. Chapman soon had his hands on Mary's inheritance and the couple, along with William, moved to Hastings. It was here that Mary first became ill, and following a return to London where Chapman became the licensee of a pub, Mary died on Christmas Day 1897. Young William was now alone in the care of his mother's murderer. At Chapman's trial, an official from Dr Barnardo's testified that on 30 January 1898 Chapman contacted them about a boy named Willie Spink. Chapman said that the boy's mother had died and he wanted him admitted into a Barnardo's home, claiming the boy had no relations. Officials tried to track down Willie's family and Mary's cousin, Joseph, later admitted at Chapman's trial that he first learnt of Mary's death when a representative from Dr Barnardo's knocked on his door. However, Joseph did not offer his kinswoman's child a home, and young Willie continued to live with Chapman and his new barmaid Bessie Taylor. In March 1899 Chapman again attempted to get rid of the boy by applying to Shoreditch workhouse. Within a short period of time, Willie was installed at the workhouse, which was just as well; it was not long before Chapman began the slow poisoning of his second victim, Bessie Taylor. William was just ten years old.

However, William did not remain in Shoreditch workhouse, because on the 1901 census he is to be found at the Cottage Homes in Hornchurch, Essex. He is described as a pauper and place of birth is 'unknown'. William was now just a statistic. This establishment was home to 358 children and had been opened in 1889 to house the pauper children of Shoreditch workhouse. It was in the style of a village street: there were eleven 'cottages', each housing thirty children. Whilst the home was overcrowded, it did boast a school, swimming bath, band room, needlework room, workshops and an infirmary. So by the standards of the day it provided a good environment. William was in the company of many children of his own age, and he received an education. We can only hope that this poor little lad found some comfort amongst his playmates and caring staff and was able to develop normally in his formative years. The children in the home were aged between four and fifteen years, so once William turned fifteen, what became of him?

There are two possibilities: the most likely is a William Spink recorded in the 1911 census. His age is given as twenty-one and he is a Private in the First Battalion Lincolnshire Regiment, posted in Aden. It would seem that this William Spink died in action, aged twenty-eight, in August 1917 in Belgium. Alternatively, there is a William Spink who departed from Liverpool bound for Quebec in June 1910. We cannot be sure what happened to our young William, but there is no doubt that this little boy was as much a victim of Jack the Ripper as his mother.

Chapman's second victim, as we have already seen, was Bessie Taylor. She too was poisoned by her 'husband' after an alleged marriage and died an agonising death on 13 February 1901 at the Monument Tavern in Southwark, where Chapman was the publican. Unlike Mary, Bessie did not have any children and had not been previously married.

Bessie was the daughter of Thomas and Betsey Taylor, who were farmers in Cheshire. She was the fourth of seven children and was born in 1862. Evidence would suggest that they were a reasonably affluent family. William, Bessie's elder brother and her parents were to be added to the list of Chapman's victims.

Bessie introduced Chapman to her brother as her husband and William had no reason to doubt that. But just like Mary Spink before her, there is no evidence that Bessie was ever married to this evil man.

William first discovered his sister's death when his distraught mother contacted him on the day of Bessie's death. Two days later William – along with Chapman and other members of Bessie's family – accompanied her coffin on its journey from St Pancras Station back to Cheshire where Bessie was laid to rest in Lymm churchyard. Unable to recover from the loss of their child, both of Bessie's parents died in the following year; her father was aged sixty-nine and her mother seventy-three. Thomas and Betsy were interred with their daughter. In the space of eighteen months, William watched three members of his family lowered into this grave, all of them victims of George Chapman.

Only three or four months later on a dark November morning, William was back in Lymm churchyard to witness the exhumation of his sister's body. After the harrowing removal of his parents' coffins, Bessie's was finally lifted from the ground. William was so distressed that it was a family friend, William Kelsal, who had to formally identify Bessie's remarkably preserved remains once the coffin was opened. There can be no doubt that William will have lived with that scene for the rest of his life, and it is to his credit that only three months later he was able to give clear and lucid evidence at Chapman's trial.

As William struggled to sleep in the days and weeks that followed the exhumation and then the trial, his thoughts will have alternated between grief and anger. Grief that his sister's life was cut short at the age of thirty-six by the hand of the very man that was supposed to love her. Grief that not only had Chapman murdered his sister, but as a consequence had taken the lives of his parents. Anger that Bessie's death certificate, and even the inscription plate on her coffin – for which William had paid – carried the name Bessie Chapman. Anger at Bessie's doctor's inability to recognise poisoning and recording 'Intestinal obstruction, vomiting and exhaustion' as the cause of death. Anger that it was to take the death of another woman before William would see justice for his sister.

The third murder victim was Maud Marsh. Maud was one of the five children, four girls and one boy, who were born to Robert and Eliza Marsh. Maud's parents and sisters were to be the next additions to the victim list.

Robert and Eliza lived at various addresses in Croydon throughout their married life. Robert Marsh was variously recorded as a carman, bricklayer and furniture dealer. By April 1901 Maud had moved out of the family home to work as a housemaid. However, the family appear to have been close-knit and supportive, and when Maud spotted the advertisement placed by Chapman for a barmaid at the Monument pub in August 1901, it was her mother who accompanied her to the interview. Maud was given the position, and within a short period of time Maud and Chapman led the Marsh family to believe that they had married. Maud kept in contact with her sisters and confided in her elder sister Louisa that Chapman had been violent towards her. By the end of July 1902, Maud was showing the symptoms that the previous 'Mrs Chapmans' had shown.

Maud's parents and sisters visited her frequently throughout her illness, and in her dying days Maud was nursed by her mother at Chapman's pub. Eliza begged Maud's doctor to do something to stop her daughter's vomiting. When the doctor confessed to being 'at his wits' end', Maud's father Robert, concerned for his daughter's life, arranged for his own doctor to give a second opinion. In fact it was this doctor that came to the conclusion that this was a case of arsenic poisoning, but his realisation came too late as Maud died the day after his visit. However, he telegraphed his suspicions to the doctor in attendance and this started the chain of events which was to lead to Chapman's arrest, trial and subsequent execution.

MAUDE MARSH.

Maud Marsh was the third murder victim of George Chapman.

Robert, Eliza and all three of Maud's sisters gave moving evidence at Chapman's trial. They had been powerless to prevent Maud's death and yet must have blamed themselves for not removing her from Chapman's clutches. Robert and Eliza would have realised as the trial progressed that their daughter's poisoning was going on right under their noses but they, like their daughter, had been taken in by this serial killer. Mrs Marsh told the jury that the day after Maud's death, Chapman suggested that her youngest daughter Alice might like to join him as his new barmaid. Naively, Alice had declined his offer. Alice Marsh could have become Chapman's fourth murder victim. It is unlikely that the Marsh family ever recovered from their ordeal. Robert and Eliza lived out their years in Croydon, Eliza dying in 1913 and Robert in 1927.

Chapman had met his wife-to-be Lucy Baderski (or Baderska) at a Polish club in Clerkenwell. After a courtship of only four or five weeks, they were married in October 1889 at St Boniface Church in Mile End. Lucy was just nineteen years old. A son was born in September 1890, but died of pneumonia some six months later. Sometime in 1891, the couple emigrated to the United States but Lucy returned to the UK in February 1892 and said that Chapman had been acting violently towards her. It is with hindsight that we can say that Lucy was lucky to escape with her life. In May 1892 Lucy gave birth to her second child, a girl they named Cecilia, at No. 26 Scarborough Street in Whitechapel, the home of Lucy's sister. Chapman returned to the UK about two weeks after Cecilia's birth and registered the birth himself on 20 June. However their reconciliation did not last long; by

November 1893 Chapman had left his wife and daughter and was living with another woman in Tottenham.

So what became of Chapman's wife Lucy and his daughter Cecilia? Their lives must have been turned upside down when Chapman was hanged for murder when the little girl was just eleven years old.

By 1901 Lucy and Cecilia were living in Limehouse with a fellow Pole, Frank, along with Lucy and Frank's son Henry who was born in April 1899. Frank and Lucy are recorded on the census as 'married'; however they were not actually married until June 1903, just two months after Chapman's execution. On their wedding certificate Lucy described herself as a widow; she was now free to marry the man she loved. In the 1911 census the couple can be forgiven for describing themselves as having been married for thirteen years, as this is obviously a reference to the length of time they had been together. On Henry's birth certificate Lucy gives her maiden name as 'Late Klosowski formerly Baderska'. Not denying her past, it would seem that Lucy was able to find happiness with Frank, and together they went onto to have a total of five children.

Cecilia left home and was married at the tender age of sixteen years and five months in October 1908. She married Albert, a thirty-one year old Pole who was a master ladies' tailor. Cecilia gave her father's name as Severin Klosowski (deceased). They too went on to have five children. Like her mother, Cecilia was able to find happiness after what must have been a traumatic childhood. It is interesting that she married a man fourteen years her senior; was this young woman looking for a stable father figure? It would seem she found one in Albert. Cecilia died in 1960 aged sixty-seven, having been a widow for ten years.

Though it is clear that both women were able to lead fulfilling lives after Chapman's trial, they were just as much victims as the families of the murdered women.

George Chapman was hanged on 7 April 1903 at HMP Prison Wandsworth. On hearing the news, Frederick George Abberline, who had investigated the Whitechapel murders of 1888

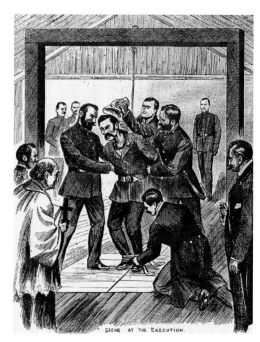

'The Hanging of George Chapman' (Illustrated Police News *18 April 1903)*

was said to have remarked 'They have caught the Ripper at last'. Chapman's murder spree was over. Innocent women were dead. His wife and daughter were able to rebuild their lives, but his victims' families lived with the pain of the death of their loved ones for many years.

All of them victims of Jack the Ripper.

Thanks to Penny Benninger for all her advice and Helena Wojtczak for correcting my mistakes.

Bibliography

Adams. H. L., *Trial of George Chapman* (Notable British Trials Series) (William Hodge & Co., 1930)

Endnote (1)

See The Whitechapel Society, *Jack the Ripper: The Suspects*, Chapter 3 (The History Press, 2011)

Susan Parry

Sue is a retired deputy head teacher of a secondary school and is now teaching mathematics part-time. She has been a member of the Whitechapel Society since the very beginning and took on the role of secretary, and later treasurer in 2006. Sue lives in Norfolk with her husband Phil, a chartered accountant. They have three children and four grandchildren.

FOUR

The Monarchical Misnomer

By Mickey Mayhew

Dedicated to Piggie, Tiggy, and the parents.

From Hell is my definitive Ripper film; it's the one that skewered my rather carefree curiosity and then hurled me headfirst into the subject. To this day I don't even know what made me go and see it in the first place. I think I caught the trailer whilst seeing something else entirely, but I remember sitting there sort of spellbound by brief glimpses of the gaslit back alleys, by the sleek images of slick, rain-spattered cobbles, and of the spectacular recreation of Christ Church on Commercial Street, even though at that point I don't think I'd ever set foot there before. The film is something of a triumph of style over substance; the less mature Mickey won over as much by the film's abundance of surface detail as the elder, more well-informed model was later to be disappointed at the lack of any real, rigorous research beneath it. That was at a time when I was first really flexing my Ripperologist biceps, seeking out the various sources to see where the story that painted the Royal Family as possible Ripper sponsors really came from. It never occurred to me on first viewing that there might be more victims in the narrative than the 'classic' canonical five (or six). Just because they weren't gutted like a fish didn't mean all the protagonists necessarily got through to the end credits with their reputations unscathed.

From Hell (the film) has the Jack the Ripper murders taking place because Queen Victoria's grandson, Prince Eddy – Prince Albert Victor, Duke of Clarence, to give him his full due – falls in love with a prostitute, whom he marries; they have a child; their wedding is witnessed by the prostitute's six friends, who are also the five – or six, if you're of a mind to count Martha Tabram – canonical victims of Jack the Ripper. The fact that a grandson of the Queen has married a prostitute, yet alone in a Catholic ceremony, is enough for her to have despatched her chief physician, Sir William Gull – a rather hellish turn by Ian Holm, if you'll pardon the pun – to sort the sorry mess out. Gull turns out to be psychotic (this was somehow overlooked by his contemporaries) and also turns out therefore to be Jack the Ripper. The women are silenced – or so Gull thinks – and then he himself is lobotomised for his troubles, thus making sure that he can never spill the Royal Family's sordid secret. Mary Kelly actually escapes her fate and flees to live out her life in anonymity, a fate she would joyfully embrace later on in Melvyn Fairclough's *The Ripper and The Royals*. Her purported places of safety are becoming so numerous that tales of her flight from fate will doubtless offer future writers of such fabricated tosh more destinations than Ryanair.

It was all new to me at the time, but *From Hell* is simply the latest in a long line of films, books, or indeed graphic novels about the Ripper coming at the subject from the royal angle (it was in fact adapted from Alan Moore's rather marvellous epic graphic novel of the same name). In fact, Prince Eddy's name was first linked to the Ripper killings in a rather roundabout way in the 1960s in a biography about Edward VII, and then by Dr Thomas Stowell when he told it to Colin Wilson. The theory exploded in the 1970s when Stowell decided to further this rather macabre game of Chinese whispers by publishing his theory in *The Criminologist*. The theory was basically – bear with me on this one – the notion that Prince Eddy (referred to as 'S' throughout but obvious enough nevertheless) was the Ripper, and that this information had been gleaned from the records of Sir William Gull, the royal physician. Stowell also claimed to have discovered that Eddy did not in fact die of the flu but of syphilis, which added some sort of fact, however feeble, to the notion that he might have been the sort of man to pursue the company of prostitutes (later on it would be alleged by Melvyn Fairclough that he

would survive these various shenanigans and see out his serial killer retirement in the relative seclusion of Glamis Castle). At this point Prince Eddy ceased rather rapidly to become the central suspect and merely became the catalyst for the crimes, as seen in *From Hell*, and basically almost every other Ripper-related feature from then on.

At roughly the same time as Stowell's theory first went public, a BBC news team who were researching for a series on the Ripper spoke to a certain Joseph Sickert about allegations surrounding his parentage. This theory was then investigated by Stephen Knight in a series of interviews which eventually spawned his best-selling book *Jack the Ripper: The Final Solution*, thus cementing the Ripper with the Royal Family for a generation and indeed beyond. This

Prince Eddy, who has become the Ripper media's 'big name draw'.

was the first book to really blow the lid on the whole thing, rivetingly readable but actually rather rubbish factually. It is with this telling that the story which would eventually become *From Hell* really begins, with Gull doing the dirty deeds, and joined by the artist Walter Sickert (father of Joseph); later on. In other versions they would be accompanied by countless other 'names' of the time, including Sir Robert Anderson, the head of CID; Robert James Lees, a rather camp – if you favour the Michael Caine TV movie – clairvoyant; and let us not forget Netley, the callous coachman. In this version poor Walter Sickert, whose reputation would be ravaged almost with a sense of relish by Patricia Cornwell several decades later, was supposedly the owner of a studio overlooking a sweet shop where one Annie Crook worked, whom Prince Eddy, when visiting Sickert at his studio, took a liking to. As I pointed out in the film of *From Hell*, Sickert, his studio and the sweet shop were all excised in favour of making Annie merely one of a gang of prostitutes that basically made up the canonical five, along with perpetual maybe-Ripper murder victim Martha Tabram.

Jack the Ripper: The Final Solution was a sensation and a bestseller, and blew the whole idea of the Ripper and the Royal Family into the public consciousness. The narrative at this point in the mid-1970s becomes positively putty in the hands of anyone wanting to make a quick buck off the connection. For instance, if Prince Eddy's marital mess wasn't being cleared up by Sir William Gull as Jack the Ripper, then it was his rather hedonistic homosexual love life that led either him or his friends – step forward James Kenneth Stephen, a tutor of Eddy's whose frustrated fantasies for the prince are played out on the unsuspecting women of Whitechapel – to become ersatz serial killers themselves (Stephen's father was also involved in the Maybrick trial, thus creating enough threads to satisfy the conspiracy theorists who crave and indeed cultivate such connections). This theory came about from a book by Michael Harrison, and later became the basis for the *Prince Jack* book, but more on that later. And so the cast grows, with the story unfolding in ways so bizarre and unreal that it seems like a metaphor for some sort of crazy criminal work of origami. And yet it all somehow seems so very essential; Prince Eddy as Jack the Ripper is something that makes the subject a little more interesting to the average man, despite the fact that the Ripper case itself remaining unsolved really ought to be enough for anyone. His mugshot is at the top of any self-respecting rogue's gallery for those hoping to glean the identity of the world's most famous serial killer. The first thing a Ripper virgin often says to me when I tell them about my hobby is, 'Wasn't he – i.e the Ripper – meant to have been one of the Royal Family?!', whereas the more likely suspects such as Cohen, Kosminski and all the others don't get much of a look in. As far as the general public are concerned, Prince Eddy is the 'big name draw' on the subject.

However, a link between the Ripper and the Royals isn't as far-fetched as it might sound. From the actual days of the Ripper case itself, when the theory was first put forward that the killer might have had some sort of medical knowledge in order to commit the crimes, it was mooted that he might have been someone from the upper echelons of society, class being something the Victorians were rather obsessed about. From then on it becomes relatively easy to link a medical man moving in society's finer circles to someone with even classier connections, and then hey presto, you have a Ripper who might rightly be a Royal, or at the very least someone who 'hangs around' in those rather haughty sort of circles. As a nation, Britain prides itself on being rather enraptured with its Royals, and especially with any sort of scandal that surrounds them; that's why we love Anne Boleyn and the questions of sorcery and sordid love trysts that surround her; that's why we're mystified by Mary Queen of Scots and the subject of whether she did indeed blow up her vicious, syphilitic bisexual husband in order to marry her bit of rough from the Borders. As a rule, the Royals are meant to be a bit above all that sort of thing, so when we find them knee-deep in the sort of naughtiness normally reserved for the lower classes, then we find the subject all but spellbinding; or as Stephen Knight found to his positive delight, a real page-turner.

In Ripperology circles where the study is both serious and scholarly the Royal suspects don't actually factor too highly in terms of credibility; they're more of an amusing side note to the more serious suspects, such as the aforementioned Cohen and Kosminski, but as I said, the Royals provide vital oxygen to what would otherwise be a comparatively niche market interest. Nowadays it's more of a question of who was a 'celebrity' name at the time of the murders who isn't now a suspect; Lewis Carroll, Sir John Williams ... the list unfolds with the same sort of weird wonder as the stories of Knight and Harrison themselves, another wacky work of weird and wonderful metaphorical origami.

The Ripper and the Royals by Melvyn Fairclough again revolves around the idea that Prince Eddy's misdemeanours were protected and then put right by a group of Royal hangers-on and handymen; the Sickerts are again involved, this time behind scenes and therefore without benefit of Walter himself serving as one of the main suspects. The foreword to the book is by Joseph Sickert, who, as I explained, was already in on the act by way of being involved in the gestation of the notorious *Final Solution* after being 'discovered' by the BBC. Supposedly cribbed in part from the secret diaries of Inspector Abberline, this book paints the hapless Prince Eddy as an almost ludicrous figure, worthy of lament rather than someone who needs lambasting; indeed, as some sort of Victorian Lily Savage: '... Eddy liked to smoke Turkish cigarettes, and he was known to be a heavy drinker; but, worse than this, by 1889 it was also becoming accepted among certain sections of society that he was bisexual. He seems to have been a familiar figure at several homosexual establishments, where he was known as "Victoria".' He ends up coming across as some sort of hapless bungler who has to be bailed out of ever-increasingly ludicrous scrapes by his set of 'straight men' (both literally and metaphorically). This version of Prince Eddy, first put sharply into focus by Stephen Knight, survives all the way to the *From Hell* graphic novel and the film adaptation that followed it, with Alan Moore giving the definitive portrayal of Eddy as some sort of feckless fop floundering in sea of East End filth. It has to be said that this final, finely crafted version of Prince Eddy was in some aspects not too far from the truth; he had been an apparently slow child with a general disinterest in learning, who grew up into a rather uninspiring adult, seeking stimulation from a variety of pursuits, some less well-advised than others. But he seems almost certain not to have been the Ripper, with alibis about being out of the country or at the very least in the wrong part of this country abounding. Donald Rumbelow, the King of Ripperology, rather deftly lambasts the Knight theory and its various bastard literary spawn, including Frank Spiering's *Prince Jack*, of which he says '... the extremes to which the Clarence theorists can go is best exemplified by Frank Spiering's *Prince Jack*. The author attempts to justify his bizarre creation by stating in the introduction that the book "is mainly a reconstruction of what I feel did happen, based on everything I read, officially and unofficially".' This isn't to say that the various Ripper/Royalty books aren't great reading and rather entertaining, but for the most part they're fodder for the masses.

However, the Royal Family at the time of the Ripper crimes is much bigger than simply Prince Eddy, and no other figure at the time loomed much larger than life than his grandmother, Queen Victoria, who also appears in both the graphic novel and the film *From Hell*, notably giving the go-ahead to clear up her grandson's grubby mess to Sir William Gull. This veritable matriarch of mourning casts a long, gloomy shadow over the events of 1888 and it seems that there was no monarch better suited to sitting on the throne at the time of

Queen Victoria and the Royal Family.

the Ripper murders than herself; one has to strain to imagine the Queen Mother, for instance, attempting to voice her concerns about East End poverty over the incessant clatter of tea and crumpets; however, had she been forced to do so, one is in no doubt that she would have come good and been able to look the people of the East End in the eye a second time. Of course in the realm of reality, Victoria actually voiced her concern about the murders, which adds fuel to the fire to any Royal conspiracy theory, with the whole 'double bluff/guilty conscience' angle coming into play. Stephen Knight cites, for once rather correctly, that '... the obsessional mourning she affected after the death in 1861 of her beloved consort Albert did much to damage her popularity. The country became irritated by her prolonged seclusion, and outraged by her obstinate refusals to take part in public events. A campaign against her social hibernation led eventually to a monarchy crisis.' She became at the most a misunderstood monarch, whose children and grandchildren were seen almost to run amok against the restrained social mores of the time. It is little wonder in some respects that the Royals at the time of the Ripper have been targeted by accusations, given the umbrella under which they were operating, in the form of this rather woeful old woman. And perhaps, to the minds of the day, the idea of the Ripper and the Royals isn't quite as far-fetched as Donald Rumbelow would have us believe; Inspector Abberline himself was purported to have said that they '... should look for the Ripper very high up in society'. That doesn't necessarily mean the Royals, but one can see how fevered minds at the time might make such a connection.

To sum it all up, Donald Rumbelow himself cites the connection between the Ripper and the Royals as Ripperology's '... perfect combination for the sensation seekers despite the ridicule that has been heaped upon the resulting theories. A comic book, with the Duke of Clarence as Jack the Ripper fighting Dracula for the love of Mary Kelly, had to be either a high or a low point in Ripperana, depending on your perspective.' I myself have heard the great man telling this very story many times, usually as one of the main punchlines to his walk around the various murder sites, deftly delivered as we stood in the remains of what was once Dorset Street. However, despite this rather damning denouement, it seems that the connection between the Ripper and the Royals is as necessary for the enterprise of Ripperology as is the fact that the Ripper's identity must actually remain secret. To discover it would be to spoil it for everyone, the way – as Quentin Crisp once said – a consumptive with a cough spoils the fun of tuberculosis. Mud sticks, and the globs masterfully slung by Messrs Stowell, Sickert, Knight et al over the years is actually so much more like a soothing balm than a source of slander; necessary, in fact, to keep this forever booming industry perpetually in bloom – think less mud, and more like manure.

Bibliography

Articles

Stowell, Dr Thomas, 'Jack the Ripper – A Solution?', *The Criminologist* (November 1970)

Books

Fairclough, Melvyn, *The Ripper and the Royals* (Duckworth, 1991)
Knight, Stephen, *Jack the Ripper: The Final Solution* (Grafton Books, 1976)
Rumblelow, Donald, *The Complete Jack the Ripper* (Penguin Books, 2004)

Films

From Hell, Hughes, Albert, and Hughes, Allan, dir. (Twentieth Century Fox, 2001)

Mickey Mayhew

Mickey is a regular contributor to the Whitechapel Society journal, as well as being a film and theatre reviewer for a London lifestyle magazine; he is currently studying for his PhD on Anne Boleyn and Mary Queen of Scots, a considerable achievement for someone thrown out of school at thirteen and earmarked for rather poor prospects. His novel *Jack and the Lad* is available on Amazon Kindle.

FIVE

The Strange Case of Dr Jekyll and Richard Mansfield

By Andrew O'Day

In the autumn of 1888 a string of brutal murders of penniless prostitutes, believed to be by the same hand, took place in the East End of London. Meanwhile, over in the West End's Lyceum Theatre, a production of Robert Louis Stevenson's *The Strange Case of Dr Jekyll and Mr Hyde* was being staged by theatre manager Henry Irving, starring American actor Richard Mansfield (born in Germany in 1857), who had first played the dual title role on Broadway. This chapter revolves around the notion that in both the print media of the late nineteenth century and the television media of the twentieth, the production of *Jekyll and Hyde* and Richard Mansfield himself was tied into the Jack the Ripper case and can be seen as victims.

The first question we must ask is this: was the production of *Jekyll and Hyde* cancelled out of fear that it was inspiring the murderer? Did the production therefore fall victim to the Ripper murders in this sense? There are different stories about this, just as there are different stories about the identity of the Ripper. Bill Doll, for example, takes an unconventional view that the Ripper murders led to the play's financial success, while conversely, Paul Begg, Martin Fido and Keith Skinner argue that the murders led to the financial failure of the play. Tom Cullen claims that the public condemnation of the play caused it to be taken off; a point which Gary Coville and

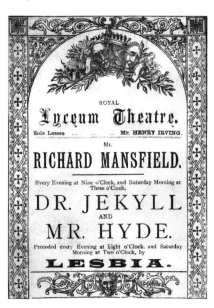

The Strange Case of Dr. Jekyll and Mr. Hyde, staged in the autumn of 1888.

Patrick Lucanio claim is echoed in Edwin Zbonek's German film *Das Ungeheuer von London City* (1964). Martin A. Danahay and Alex Chisholm note that 'the impetus that persuaded Mansfield to close *Jekyll and Hyde* ... was financial rather than due to any second thoughts about performing during the Ripper scare'.

What is clear, however, is that the production of *Jekyll and Hyde* fell victim to the media frenzy of the day surrounding the Ripper murders. In this time of New Journalism, the newspapers of the day were quick to sensationalise the connections between the Ripper killings and *Jekyll and Hyde*. For example, the edition from 1 September 1888 of *The Globe* alluded to the story: 'One can almost imagine that Whitechapel is haunted by a demon of the type of Hyde, who goes about killing for the mere sake of slaughter'. The *Irish Times* of 7 September 1888 stated that 'the Whitechapel murder has taken a turn of most ghastly romance. Those ... will remember how the horrible Hyde in one of his transformations, butcher-ed a woman just for the fun of the thing ... His visage perpetually set in a malignant grin, and his sinister eye ... are enough to give a nervous person fits'. The *Pall Mall Gazette* of 8 September 1888 also alluded to the story, stating that 'there certainly seems to be a tolerably realistic impersonation of Mr Hyde at large in Whitechapel'. That same day, the *East London Advertiser* speculated that perhaps the murderer materialised at night 'like another Hyde to prey upon the defenceless women of the "unfortunate" class'. The *Star* of 11 September 1888 meanwhile, quotes an 'eccentric correspondent' who writes that 'the murderer is a Mr Hyde, who seeks in the repose and comparative respectability of Dr Jekyll security from the crimes he commits in his baser shape'. Again, *The Star* on 14 September 1888 noted that 'Mysterious personages flit through ... like the shadowy and awful figures in Poe's and Stevenson's novels'. Also on that date, the *Pall Mall Gazette* asked whether the savage yet skilful acts of the killer did not 'point rather to Mr Hyde than to a wandering lunatic?' Making the connection with Mansfield's performance, the *Pall Mall Gazette* of 4 October 1888 printed:

> Possibly the culprit is an army doctor suffering from sunstroke. He has seen the horrible play, lives in Bayswater or North London, in perhaps a decent square or terrace, dressed well. Goes out about 10pm straight to Whitechapel. Commits deed. Home again to breakfast. Wash, brush-up, sleep. Himself again ... Meantime, everybody scouring the scene of the tragedy for the usual type of a murderer.

Coville and Lucanio in their book *Jack the Ripper: His Life and Crimes in Popular Entertainment* point out that Cullen quotes from the *Daily Telegraph*: 'Experience has taught ... that there is no taste in London now for horrors on the stage. There is quite sufficient to make us shudder out of doors'. The newspapers claimed that Mansfield wisely went on to work in a different genre, comedy, in his revival of A.C. Gunter's

Prince Karl, as a benefit performance to raise money for reformed prostitutes.

What is also certain is that suspicion was briefly cast in the newspapers as to whether Richard Mansfield was the Ripper, and in this respect Mansfield can be seen as having been a victim. As Danahay and Chisholm write in *Jekyll and Hyde Dramatized: The 1887 Richard Mansfield Script and the Evolution of the Story on Stage*, 'thanks to Richard Mansfield's compelling portrayal of Dr Jekyll's transformation into Mr Hyde, the actor was denounced as a suspect in the Ripper murders'. 'The letter denouncing Mansfield as the Ripper', Danahay and Chisholm continue, 'claims, in poor spelling, that "I do not think there is A man Living So well able to disguise Himself in A moment as he does in front of the Public".' Suspicion was cast on people in particular groups, such as butchers

Mansfield's portrayal of Jekyll and Hyde. Suspicion was briefly cast in the newspapers as to whether Richard Mansfield was the Ripper.

(who made a living with a knife) and doctors (who would have been aware of how to remove the victims' organs with surgical skill). The finger was also pointed at Mansfield, not because of any real evidence against him, but solely because he was playing the part of Mr Hyde.

While we do not know the motivation of this newspaper letter-writer, the letter can certainly be placed in the context of the frenzy that the Jack the Ripper murders generated. The finger was pointed at foreigners and Jews, and the Whitechapel Vigilance Committee (led by Mr George Lusk) took to the streets at night in search of the killer. The majority of the hysteria, however, was to be found in the print media of the day. For example, newspapers made the connection between the Whitechapel Murderer and Mr Hyde (as noted above) and The *Illustrated Police News* sensationalised events, calling the killer a 'monster' more generally, both of which unintentionally implicated Mansfield.

Additionally, Danahay and Chisolm relate a little anecdote in relation to the Jekyll and Hyde play. They explain that on 29 September 1888 the St Stephen's Review reported: 'Between the Whitechapel murders and the weird performance of Dr Jekyll and Mr Hyde, the mental condition of people with highly-strung nerves is becoming very serious'. The writer elaborates that he was attracted by a crowd in the Strand the other night, and on investigating the matter, found that they surrounded a well-dressed young man who had bolted out of a bus while it was going at a rapid rate, and then fallen down in a fit. It appeared he had been to see Mr Mansfield as Dr Jekyll, and on getting into the bus found himself beside a most repulsive-looking man, whom he immediately concluded must either be the Doctor himself or the Whitechapel murderer.

It was 'in a fit of fearful nervousness' that 'he jumped from his seat, and came to grief'.

Furthermore, Jekyll and Hyde and Mansfield have come down to us as victims of the Ripper murders through the modern media. The main production which highlights this is David Wickes' 1988 miniseries *Jack the Ripper*. Before looking at that, it is important to examine Wickes' background, the genesis of the miniseries and its genre. Wickes' career is interesting since he started off as a documentarian and then went on to become a dramatist. In the commentary on the *Jack The Ripper*

The American actor Richard Mansfield, who had first played the dual title role of Jekyll and Hyde on Broadway.

Special Edition DVD, Wickes reveals that he had, for a long time, been in the care of Lloyd Shirley, Head of Documentaries at ABC (later to become Thames Television), and that Shirley allowed him to make the transition to drama, where he made series like *Public Eye* (1965–75), *Special Branch* (1969–74), and *The Sweeney* (1974–78). Wickes worked for Euston Films, a subsidiary company of Thames Television which was established in 1971 and was devoted to producing drama, while there were other companies for other genres such children's animation. Furthermore, in 1973, Wickes was involved in directing a series of six fifty-minute episodes called *Jack The Ripper* for the BBC which featured Superintendents Barlow and Watt from *Z Cars* (1962–78) and *Softly, Softly* (1966–69). Wickes talks about how he pitched the idea for a miniseries on Jack the Ripper to Shirley, who had by now become Head of Drama, and was given the go-ahead to make a three-hour special by David Elstein, Controller at Thames Television. Originally starring Barry Foster as Inspector Frederick Abberline, this production was far more scaled-down than the one which eventually made the screen. It had a quarter of the budget and was mostly shot on cheaper videotape, with what location material there was to be filmed on 16mm film. Elsewhere, Wickes comments:

During this period, a friend of mine, who was the head of Lorimar in the States, called and asked if I'd like to go there to direct a film of Doctor Jekyll & Mr Hyde. I told him I couldn't because I was doing Jack the Ripper and he said, 'Oh my God, David, fuck Jekyll & Hyde, let's do Jack the Ripper!' I said we couldn't because we'd already been filming for ten days. Then my friend said he thought he could get it on CBS. (See Sothcott, undated)

In the DVD documentary, Wickes reveals that CBS were enthusiastic about the idea, but were reluctant to go ahead with an unknown actor in a leading role.

CBS agreed that if Thames Television put up some money, they would put up the rest. Filming on the original version was immediately halted in October 1987 by David Elstein, Lloyd Shirley, and Wickes, and many of the actors were replaced. It was a real coup to get A-list star Michael Caine to replace Barry Foster as Abberline, since it was widely felt that Caine, living in the States at the time, 'did not do television'. Performers who were 'accredited ratings-pullers' were added to the list, including Jane Seymour (who was tempted by the fact that as large a star as Caine was involved) and Armand Assante as Richard Mansfield. The eventual budget for the miniseries was about $11 million, with slightly more than half the money coming from the United States and the rest from Thames, with the miniseries fitting within Euston Films' remit to produce filmed high-quality drama to be shown nationally on the ITV network (*see* Alvarado and Stewart 1985 for further reading on Euston Films).

The 1988 production can be described as a docudrama. Derek Paget in *No Other Way to tell it: Dramadoc/Docudrama on Television* quotes British playwright and essayist David Edgar who noted that, 'In documentary drama ... the doc is merely a means to the dram'. Concerning this particular miniseries, while it is quite clear from the DVD commentary that Sue Davies spent four years (1983–87) researching the Whitechapel murders, Wickes talks about having taken 'dramatic license' with certain events, stating 'We need to have a drama here, not only a history book', and 'We are in the business, not doing a sombre virtuous documentary that no one wants to watch'. As Coville and Lucanio point out, Donald Rumbelow stated for a 1995 Arts and Entertainment Network biography of Jack the Ripper that 'the whole thing, 99 per cent of it, is fiction'.

In Wickes' miniseries, the sensation which Richard Mansfield's transformation from Jekyll to Hyde created in the theatre audience is clearly depicted, and it is later stated that Jekyll and Hyde was taken off for fear that it was inspiring the killings. Mansfield laments that he no longer gets to play his monster as he ends up playing to half-empty houses. The production of Jekyll and Hyde is laboured on in the miniseries, however, to tell a good fictional 'story'. As it turns out, Sir William Gull is unmasked as 'Jack the Ripper', whose motivation for killing five prostitutes was to understand his half-sane, half-insane mind – though not through drinking a potion, a notion he scoffs at. Therefore, the killer had 'two faces'; a symbolic picture which clairvoyant Robert James Lees had earlier given Abberline.

Furthermore, Mansfield can be regarded as a 'victim' in other exaggerated ways. In an outstanding talk given at the 2011 Whitechapel Society conference, Professor Clive Bloom highlighted the notion of Jack the Ripper as being a role, or as he put it, fitting into a narrative pattern which was largely gothic. There is, according to Bloom, a big difference between the real-life 'perpetrator' of these horrendous crimes and the 'mythic structure' in which Jack the Ripper is frequently presented. For example, Bloom spoke of how cinematic productions often place the Ripper dressed in a coat and deerstalker cap in a claustrophobic and threatening mise-en-scene of brick walls and of streets shrouded in night-time fog. These are constructions, since as Bloom noted, the Ripper killings took place on clear nights. Bloom highlighted that Jack the Ripper can be taken out of his time and placed in a variety of scenes, such as in German Expressionistic films of the 1920s, characterised by conjuring up mood through shadows cast on walls and jagged shapes, and can even be depicted as the vampiric Count Dracula. In another pertinent talk for the Whitechapel Society, this time in 2012, Clare Smith also spoke of the iconography associated with the Ripper in film: the way in which he is frequently dressed in a top hat with a Gladstone bag signifying his association with the West End and the medical profession. But this idea of constructed characters does not stop with the Ripper himself; it also extends to figures whose identity is known, such as Abberline (*see* Clare Smith's chapter in this volume) and Richard Mansfield.

In the 1988 production, Mansfield is presented as an arrogant man who frequents posh brothels, riding along the streets of the East End in a carriage, picking up prostitutes off the streets, and who also tries his luck in the local pubs (including on one occasion, picking up Mary Jane Kelly). Mansfield is, moreover, presented as a prime suspect in the case far more than in his day. He is 'victimised' by the police, Inspector Abberline and Sergeant Godley, in a highly exaggerated manner. In this instance, Inspector Abberline in particular bears a grudge against Mansfield because of the actor's romantic involvement with Abberline's ex-love, Emma Prentiss. Abberline tells her to never be alone with him. This is a totally fabricated plot, as there is no evidence that Abberline even met Emma Prentiss, let alone was romantically involved with her. Drama, including television drama, revolves around conflict, and here Abberline and Mansfield are pitted against one another. Moreover, Mansfield (along with clairvoyant Robert James Lees) is a victim of public hysteria; the two are prevented from leaving the police station (where they have been questioned) by an angry vegetable-throwing public, and must be rescued by journalist Ben Bates, who has a carriage waiting for them. In this way, Mansfield is treated like butchers, who are also on as victims of public hysteria with rocks thrown through their windows (as noted earlier). Such is the power of film and television that it is portrayals like this one of Richard Mansfield that remain with the viewer.

In conclusion, it is evident that being associated with the Jack the Ripper case did not harm Mansfield's professional or personal life, and so he was certainly not a victim in that respect. After the Ripper murders Mansfield returned to the United States where he not only acted in plays on Broadway by such momentous figures as Shakespeare, George Bernard Shaw, and Henrik Ibsen, but also worked as a theatre manager. In 1892 he married actress Beatrice Cameron and eventually died in 1907 from liver cancer. Mansfield can be regarded as a victim in that he is largely remembered because of his association with the the Ripper case, but the extent of that association is exaggerated by Wickes' 1988 miniseries.

Bibliography

Books

Alvarado, M., Stewart, J., *Made for Television: Euston Films Limited* (BFI, 1985)
Begg, P., Fido, M., Skinner, K., *The Complete Jack the Ripper* (John Blake, 2010)
Coville G., Lucanio P., *Jack the Ripper: His Life and Crimes in Popular Entertainment* (McFarland, 1999)
Cullen, T., *Autumn of Terror: Jack the Ripper His Crimes and Times* (Bodley Head, 1965)
Curtis, L. P., *Jack the Ripper and the London Press* (Yale University Press, 2001)
Danahay, M., Chisholm, A., *Jekyll and Hyde Dramatized: the 1887 Richard Mansfield Script and the Evolution of the Story on Stage* (McFarland, 2005)
Doll, B., Jack the Ripper (Frederick Fell, 1960)
Jones, S., *The Illustrated Police News: London's Court Cases and Sensational Stories* (Wicked Publications, 2002)
Paget, D., *No Other Way to Tell it: Dramadoc/Docudrama on Television* (Manchester University Press, 1998)

Films

Jack The Ripper, David Wickes, dir. (various, 1988)

Newspapers

East London Advertiser, 8 September 1888
The Irish Times, 7 September 1888
Pall Mall Gazette, 8 September 1888; 14 September 1888; 4 October 1888
The Globe, 1 September 1888
The Star, 11 September 1888; 14 September 1888

Other

Bloom, C., 'Jack the Ripper at the Movies' (Whitechapel Society Conference, 1 October 2011)
Smith, C., 'Top Hat, Gladstone Bag and Fog: Jack the Ripper – Creating the iconography of a Monster on screen' (Whitechapel Society, 2 June 2012)

Websites

Sharp, A., 'The Strange Case of Dr Jekyll and Saucy Jacky' (http://www.casebook.org/dissertations/rip-alansharp.html)

Sothcott, J., 'Jack the Ripper', Action TV, 1988 (http://www.startrader.co.uk/Action%20TV/articles/jtr.htm)

Williams, J., 'Euston Films' (Screen Online, http://www.screenonline.org.uk/tv/id/1133069/)

Andrew O'Day

Andrew received his PhD in Television Studies from Royal Holloway, University of London for a thesis on telefantasy. His main specialism is *Doctor Who*, but he has also given talks on Jack the Ripper at conferences and is a regular contributor for the Whitechapel Society Journal, where he has written both on television productions of Jack the Ripper and Ripper Walking Tours. He can be found on the web at www.hrvt.net/andrewoday

SIX

Carrie Brown and Ameer Ben Ali

By Alfred Beadle

The first edition of the *Jack the Ripper A to Z* lists over ninety named suspects. In the twenty years since it was published, probably another twenty have emerged, giving us in excess of over 100 men and women who at one time or another have been accused of committing the East End murders of 1888.

This means that even if the killer is actually amongst them, over 100 innocent people have been branded with these crimes; over 100 miscarriages of justice. Happily nobody has ever been dragged kicking and screaming their innocence to the scaffold, at least not as the Ripper, but nonetheless their names have been besmirched and their posthumous reputations traduced.

In no case is this more harrowing and shaming than that of Ameer Ben Ali, who in 1891 was found guilty of the murder of prostitute Carrie Brown in New York City on the night of 23 April of that year. But hold on, 1891 ... New York ... what on earth has this got to do with Jack the Ripper and Whitechapel?

The story begins two-and-a-half years earlier, at the height of the London crimes. Thomas F. Byrnes was Detective Bureau chief of the NYPD. His name was ultimately to become a byword for corruption and police brutality. When he retired, he had amassed a personal fortune estimated at between $350 and $500,000 (up to $25 million in today's values). This was on a salary of $5,000 per annum. Byrnes is credited with having invented the 'third degree', for both suspects and witnesses, and his near-perfect conviction rate was due to confessions obtained by torture and beatings. Heaven knows how many innocent people he sent to gaol, but one of them was certainly Ameer Ben Ali.

With the world agog at what was going on in the streets and alleys of London's East End, Byrnes was asked by a reporter for the British newspaper *The Star*[1] how he would go about catching the Ripper if he ever came to New York. Puffing out his chest, Byrnes first proclaimed that the London police did not know what they were doing, and then said that he would have the perpetrator within forty-eight hours. Ameer Ben Ali may have read of this claim; he may even have applauded it. What he did not and could not have known, was that he and Chief Byrnes were now on a collision course decreed by a capricious fate.

On the night of 23 April 1891 Caroline 'Carrie' Brown took a man back to the East River Hotel on the Lower East Side of Manhattan. Brown is perhaps the saddest of the women whose deaths have been associated with Jack the Ripper. Aged fifty-six,[2] she was a former actress, known locally as 'Old Shakespeare'. The widow of a sea captain, she was an alcoholic who sold her faded charms for drink money.

The following morning Edward Fitzgerald,[3] the night clerk of the hotel, was routinely engaged in ensuring that the overnight guests vacated their rooms. Getting no

Thomas F Byrnes. The New York Chief of Detectives proclaimed that the London police did not know what they were doing.

answer from number 31 on the fifth floor, he used his pass key to unlock the door. What he saw in the room's dim half-light sent him reeling back in shock. Sources disagree on whether Carrie Brown lay on the bed or the floor, but there is no divergence about the awfulness of the sight which greeted Fitzgerald. In the words of the subsequent indictment against Ameer Ben Ali, Carrie had been strangled both manually and with a piece of cloth knotted tightly around her throat. She had also been disembowelled with a knife. The autopsy report, discovered only comparatively recently, confirms part of her intestines were cut out and left on the bed along with her left ovary. In addition to the 3in abdominal incision there were a number of other cuts to the genital area, plus the killer had carved an 'x' into her left buttock. Similarly an 'x' had been carved into the wall next to the door. The knife, described as a wooden-handled table knife with three notches carved on either side, was found on the floor. The blade was dull and broken; only 4in of it remained, and this had been ground to a murderous point.

A search of the surrounding rooms revealed a bowl of bloody water in room 32 (there was no bowl in the murder room), and blood on a small trapdoor leading to the roof.

It was inevitable that the first question reporters would ask was whether this was a Jack the Ripper murder. Coroner Schulze, who had already made a preliminary examination of the body in situ, fanned the flames: 'I believe that this case is the same as those of London ... I do not see any reason to suppose that the crimes may not have been committed by the fiend of London'.

Carrie Brown was a former actress, known locally as 'Old Shakespeare'.

The next morning, screaming headlines announced Jack's arrival in America.

Grinding his teeth in the background was Chief Byrnes. He had never expected to be called upon to make good his 1888 boast. If he failed, the pens in the hand of the reporters would turn into hatchets.

The key to solving the case swiftly appeared to lie with a woman named Mary Miniter. Variously described as a prostitute, drug addict and the hotel's assistant housekeeper, Miniter was the only person to have seen Carrie and her client when they had arrived. The man had registered in the name of 'C. Kinicio.' He was around 5ft 8in, in his early thirties with a long, sharp nose, and blonde moustache. He was wearing a dark brown overcoat, dark trousers and a battered derby hat. Miniter thought he might be German.

Detectives discovered that earlier on that evening, Brown had been in the company of a man known as 'Frenchy' at another flophouse. According to the manager, Mamie Harrington, Frenchy was a man to be feared and would likely use a knife. Staff also claimed to know Frenchy back at the East River Hotel, saying that he had in fact stayed there on the night of the murder. Late in the evening of 24 April, Frenchy was arrested. His name was Ameer Ben Ali, and he was actually an Algerian.

Ben Ali initially denied being with Carrie on the evening of 23 April and staying the night at the hotel, but later admitted having slept with her the previous night. He also confessed to having slept in room 33 of the hotel on the night of the murder, but vehemently disclaimed having been with Brown in room 31 or knowing anything about her death. Crucially, Mary Miniter said he was not Carrie's companion.

Even so, the police refused to let Ameer go. Instead, they detained him as a 'material witness'.

Meanwhile, hatchets were already being sharpened for Chief Byrnes. The 26 April came and went without the forty-eight-hour arrest he had once promised. The next day, the *Brooklyn Eagle* attacked him in a devastating editorial.

For a man who professes to have so much confidence in his ability, Inspector Byrnes betrays singular evidence of weakness. It is very certain that he talks too much. He has seen fit to name the perpetrator of this horrible murder in New York and has not been slow to ventilate his theories in the public prints, but it does not appear that he has done anything to warrant his estimate of his work. Less promise and more performance would be a good motto for the Inspector to heed.

Byrnes' immediate response was to become enticed by a theory that the culprit was actually Ben Ali's cousin, a will-o'-the-wisp character dubbed 'Frenchy two' by the press.

This however proved to be a dead end. It was then that Byrnes decided that his bird-already-in-the-bush, Ameer Ben Ali, was his New York Ripper. Otherwise he was looking at the derailment of his gravy train. It was as simple, as arbitrary and as cold-blooded as that.

Byrnes' detectives began to make derogatory remarks about the witnesses they were holding. Reports carefully placed in the media, questioned Mary Miniter's character and reliability. The witnesses as a whole were branded 'a drunken lot without enough intelligence to remember how the man looked'. Suffice to say that he did not look too much like Ameer.

Thus the framing of an innocent man was set in motion.

It is now time for the entrance of that hardy perennial of the miscarriage of justice, the gaol house nark singing his insidious little song in the expectation of getting favourable treatment from the authorities. In his compendium of 560 wrongful convictions, American author Jay Robert Nash lists case after wearying case in which prison informers have falsely testified against a person subsequently found to be innocent. In Ben Ali's case he was taken to Queens County Gaol on 29 April to be identified as a man who had served time there for vagrancy. This of course had very little to do with the murder of Carrie Brown, but was handy for a pair of inmates, David Galloway and Edward Smith, to come forward with a story that whilst there, Ben Ali had been in possession of a knife similar to that used to eviscerate her. The officer who had arrested him for vagrancy, Constable James Hiland, was later to give evidence that Ben Ali had had no such weapon on him.

But worse, much worse, was to follow on 30 April in the form of a leak, said to have come from the New York Health Department, but almost certainly Byrnes, to the effect that on 24 April detectives had found a trail of blood leading across the hallway from room 31 to room 33 – Ben Ali's room. There were bloodstains on both sides of the door of number 33, on a chair, the bedframe and the bedding. A Dr Edson of the Board of Health claimed that scientific analysis of the blood proved that it was human. This, no doubt, came as a surprise to the rest of the scientific community, as there was no reliable test to distinguish human blood from animal blood in 1891. Moreover, newspaper reporters had enjoyed access to room 31 and the fifth floor, but none of them had noticed these telltale blood drops.

Now the piece-de-résistance. Another expert, Dr Formand, backed by Edson and a Doctor Flint, claimed to have found blood on Ameer's socks and under his fingernails, containing food particles which could have come from Carrie's abdominal injuries.

Chief Byrnes' diagnosis of the crime now underwent a metamorphosis. 'C Kinicio' was simply an innocent client who had sex with Brown and then left the hotel, after which Ben Ali had crept into her room and killed her whilst robbing her.

There were many holes in this Swiss cheese scenario. Why had no one seen 'Kinicio' leaving the hotel, unless he was the killer after all and had exited from the roof entrance?

Otherwise, one would have expected Carrie to have left with him. She was a prostitute and an alcoholic, and if the client was not paying her for the night then she would have gone in search of more business; if he was, she would have hit the bars with her earnings.

Then there were those curious bloodstains on the trapdoor, and the bloody water in room 32. The police were now contending that Ben Ali had left the hotel by normal means after the crime. So having gone to all the trouble of laying a false trail, implying that the murderer left by the roof, he then failed to carry out the most elementary task of clearing up the blood leading from room 31 to 33, and the stains in 33. Plus, if he had then gone to 32 to use the washbowl, why was there not a second trail of blood from 33 to 32?

Despite all these unanswered questions, Ameer Ben Ali was arraigned for murder on 30 April. His trial commenced on 24 June and lasted until 10 July. The District Attorney himself led for the prosecution. Ameer's *pro bono* defence was handled by the firm Levy, Friend and House.

Much of the prosecution evidence consisted of no more than innuendo and character assassination. Witnesses painted a bleak picture of Ameer as a vicious ne'er-do-well who had been down and out in Liverpool and London (hint, hint) before arriving in America. He was branded a danger to women, and it was claimed that he had threatened to kill Carrie on a previous occasion. A burned-down tallow candle, said to have come from room 33, was produced as evidence that he had waited for her client to leave. He had been observed to 'slink' out of the hotel in a 'guilty' manner at around 5 a.m. on 24 April.

After the trial, witnesses spoke of wholesale coercion by the police. Said one: 'One dick kept hitting me in the face with a wet mop until I agreed to say terrible things in court about Frenchy'.

According to newspaper reports, Byrnes had ordered his detectives to 'pound the right story' out of the witnesses they brought to court.

But the prosecution did not have it all their own way. Attorney House scored some useful points for the defence. Mary Miniter, for instance, was forced to admit that she had made the name 'Kinicio' up; the man had not registered, she had not taken any notice of what he looked like, and the description that she gave to the police was a concoction.

Mr House was likewise able to make inroads into the forensic evidence. Defence experts doubted that the particles found in the blood had come from Carrie's intestinal wounds. They also dismissed the State's explanation of how the blood had gotten under Ben Ali's fingernails and on his socks.

All in all it was a useful job of work which divided the jury. They reached a compromise verdict acquitting Ameer of first degree murder (which carried the death penalty) and finding him guilty of murder in the second. Sent to Sing Sing prison, he was eventually placed in an asylum for the criminally insane at Matteawan (now a part of Beacon, New York).

Thankfully he was not to remain there. Reporters who had covered the case from the outset were convinced that there was something very wrong about this prosecution. In addition to the problematic blood drops between rooms 31 and 33, the bloodstains on the outside and inside of door 33 were wholly inconsistent with the fact that there was no blood on the doorknob or lock of 31. How could it be on one without the other?

Even so, it took eleven long years of diligent hard work before a bulky file supporting Ameer's innocence ended up on the desk of New York Governor Benjamin Odell. Governor Odell was to describe the affidavits in it as coming from 'people of credit'. The file contained much new evidence not given at the trial. Odell decided to pardon Ben Ali, who then slipped back to his native Algeria and out of the pages of history.

Who did kill Carrie Brown? That we shall never know for sure. About the one thing we can be reasonably certain of is that it was not Ameer Ben Ali.

If this murder taken place in East London in the Autumn of 1888 then it is likely that it would have been considered a Ripper crime, even allowing for the fact that Carrie's throat was not cut. A serial killer's signature – in the Ripper's case, genital mutilation – remains constant, but his *modus operandi* will vary according to circumstance. On the surface there was an interesting link between the murders of Carrie Brown and Catharine Eddowes. Eddowes had crosses carved on both cheeks of her face, while Carrie had an 'x' carved into the left cheek of her buttocks. The police might well have found this convincing in Whitechapel in 1888.

But this was not Whitechapel 1888, and I am inclined to think that the killing of Caroline Brown was the work of a dangerously unbalanced loner who had studied reports of the Ripper crimes and become obsessed by them. It is intriguing that he also left an 'x' on the wall of room 31, just as the Ripper was alleged to have placed a message on a wall in Goulston Street.

During the hunt for evidence to exonerate Ben Ali, it came to light that a New Jersey farmhand had left behind him a bloodstained shirt and a brass key stamped '31'when he had quit his job not long after Carrie's murder. The key matched those in use at the East River Hotel, and the man had been away from the farm at the time of the crime.

But if Carrie Brown was not a victim of Jack the Ripper, Ameer Ben Ali was. He fell prey to a corrupt and vainglorious police officer who needed a fast conviction of a killer whose crime resembled the Ripper's. In the end Ben Ali was lucky to escape with his life.

Footnotes

1. Another source gives the newspaper as *The Sun*.
2. Death certificate
3. Sources are divided between Edward Fitzgerald and Edward Harrington but the latter may be confusion with Mamie Harrington who ran the other lodging house mentioned here.

Bibliography

Books

Begg, Paul, Fido, Martin, and Skinner, Keith, *The Jack the Ripper A to Z*, (Headline Books, 1991)
Nash, Jay Robert, 'I am Innocent!' (Da Capo Press, 2008)

Websites

Barbee, Larry, 'An Investigation into the Carrie Brown murder,' 'Jack the Ripper Casebook', http://www.casebook.org/dissertations/dst-carrieb.html
Conlon, Michael, 'A Tale of Two Frenchys' http://www.casebook.org/dissertations/dst-frenchys.html
Conlon, Michael, 'The Carrie Brown Murder Case: New Revelations,' 'Jack the Ripper Casebook', http://www.casebook.org/dissertations/rip-carriebrown.html
Vanderlinden, Wolf, 'The New York Affair' Part II, 'Jack the Ripper Casebook', http://www.casebook.org/dissertations/rn-nya2.html

William Beadle

William is the former Chair of the Whitechapel 1888 Society and now the honorary Vice President. He is the author of *Jack the Ripper: Anatomy of a Myth* (1995) and *Jack the Ripper Unmasked* (2009).

He is also a member of Mensa and several other societies; Dealey Plaza (Kennedy Assassination), Richard 111, the Victorian Military Society and the Anglo-Zulu War Society.

SEVEN

Monro's Hot Potato? The Irish Angle

By Adrian Morris

'We have always found the Irish a bit odd. They refuse to be English.'

Winston Churchill

On 17 September 1888, a preliminary hearing of a parliamentary commission at the Palace of Westminster held its first sitting. This commission had been set up largely to investigate the affairs and activities of the Irish Parliamentary Party (IPP). Accusations and criticism of the IPP had been levelled against it as the agrarian unrest in Ireland had intensified in the face of the Conservative government's increasingly draconian policies in Ireland that had, ironically, tried to quell this unrest.

By the mid-1880s, agricultural prices were seriously depressed. This hit the Irish economy especially hard, considering its economic base was largely agricultural. Furthermore, the national and cultural trauma of the Great Famine of the 1840s had aggravated Irish sensibilities towards successive British governments and their system of management and administration of the economy, personified in Irish minds by the avaricious absentee landlord. From the 1870s onwards, as the prospects of Ireland's rural economy weakened, unrest by Irish tenant farmers had increased dramatically. These acts grew into a widespread and concerted campaign against authority during the Cogadh na Talún (Land Wars).

The Plan of Campaign was a rural-based initiative started in 1886 to counter the negative effects of the depression in the Irish agricultural market. The Irish National League, a domestic power base for the wider IPP, had essentially organised this initiative on behalf of the tenant farmers. In so doing, they had alienated themselves from the leading lights in the IPP.

Whilst the IPP was led by the pragmatic and politically astute Charles Stewart Parnell, many within the same party, such as the passionate and radical Michael Davitt, often aligned themselves to more extreme groups in Irish society that took a starker view of the issues facing the country. The IPP was a broad church; its chief aim, by 1888, was ultimately Home Rule for Ireland. The tectonic plates of British politics had also moved towards an agenda forged by Britain's 'oldest colony'. Home Rule was to be the issue that would divide and rule the governing parliamentary parties at Westminster. This polarisation at Westminster and beyond had become reinforced by William Gladstone's long and arduous conversion to the stance of Home Rule for Ireland in 1885. The resulting legislation by Gladstone's Liberal government, the Government of Ireland Bill 1886 was defeated by just thirty votes, but the political landscape had altered. Parliamentary politics would be set on a course for the next generation: Irish independence or the defence of the United Kingdom.

By 1888 Gladstone's administration had been defeated and a new Conservative government, led by Lord Salisbury, was in power. Moreover, Salisbury had a full majority and could follow his own agenda. A major part of this agenda would be complete and utter adherence to the Unionist cause. Salisbury's party had been augmented at Westminster by the breakaway faction from Gladstone's rump party, the self-styled Liberal Unionist Party led by a former leader of the Liberals, Lord Hartington. It included the radical Joseph Chamberlain. This new Liberal Unionist Party delivered Salisbury a sound majority, but they still occupied the opposition benches, declining to consummate a full working coalition.

This new Unionist bloc at Westminster had turned parliamentary politics on its head. It had been the solid and influential bloc of Irish MPs that had been kingmakers in the past. Parnell's Irish MPs would gravitate to the more amenable Liberal Party of Gladstone and had predominantly supported previous Gladstone governments (despite a brief flirtation with Salisbury's Conservative administration in 1885) when neither the Liberals nor Conservatives could rule outright. Understandably the Conservatives, and especially Salisbury, who was a Unionist to his very soul, would not entertain the agenda of the IPP. By 1888 they did not need to, and this would show itself with that administration's severe policy towards the rebellious Irish.

With a full mandate and without any real regard for Parnell's political agenda, Salisbury's government could deal with the Irish problem in a way that it felt would solve the problem once and for all. Salisbury was not blind to the need for reforms in the Irish rural economy; however, the appointment of his nephew, Arthur Balfour, as the Chief Secretary of Ireland was a sign that the Plan of Campaign was going to be countered in more dramatic ways.

By 1887 the Plan of Campaign had intensified and become more violent, to the political chagrin of Parnell and his hope of widening the appeal of Home Rule to more moderate and affluent supporters. Balfour passed the Coercion Act 1887 in Ireland, which declared virtual martial law. The National League became a banned organisation, and arrest of agitators was a projected aim without the need for a trial.

One of those arrested under The Stark conditions of the Coercion Act was to be the Irish MP and editor of the now banned Nationalist newspaper *The United Irishman*, William O'Brien. O'Brien had been arrested with fellow Irish politician, John Mandeville during a bloody skirmish in Mitchelstown, Co. Cork in September 1887. What had started out as the organisation of a rent strike and demonstration descended into a murderous attack by the Royal Irish Constabulary.

O'Brien's continued incarceration into November of that year, and his lack of co-operation with the prison authorities, made him a *cause célèbre* in Britain as well as Ireland. The more radical elements in the poverty stricken East End of London

William O'Brien, the Irish MP and editor of the Nationalist newspaper The United Irishman.

– their ranks swollen by the urban unemployed – decided to march in honour of their imprisoned Irish comrades, and in November 1887 a large march left the East End heading towards central London to highlight the cause of O'Brien and his fellow detainees. The event would ultimately become known as Bloody Sunday.

The new Commissioner of the Metropolitan Police Service, Sir Charles Warren, was a former soldier with all the rigidity that that brought to the job. He had been employed to deal with 'the mob' as it was seen, despite, ironically, Warren being a Gladstonian Liberal with a reformist outlook. He nevertheless indulged the desire to come down hard on a 'mob' that had, the previous year, marched from the East End to the West End causing widespread panic, mayhem and damage. Warren was not going to let this happen again and forced the march into the confines of Trafalgar Square, only to quell the demonstration through use of mounted police favouring heavy-handed methods. One demonstrator died as a result with many more injured.

Warren had won the favour of his political masters, but the radical elements, as they pulled back to the East End bloodied and bruised, were angry and unbowed. Their day to bloody Warren was not far off. They only had to wait until the autumn of the following year; a bizarre and unlikely series of murders would provide them with their opportunity.

Warren didn't see eye to eye with his political overmaster in Whitehall. Henry Matthews was the Home Secretary in Lord Salisbury's government. He was an

Irish Roman Catholic in a strongly Unionist cabinet. Matthews had been sympathetic to the Irish case for independence in his younger career, but by 1888 he was well in the Unionist camp. The Irish nationalists would despise him and hanker for a good opportunity to attack him.

Warren would find working with the pusillanimous Matthews almost impossible during the crisis both offices experienced as a result of the Whitechapel murders, which invited criticisms from all quarters. This convinced Warren that the Home Secretary's office was unable or unwilling to protect him from them. Also, wider structural issues were at play. Warren, being head of the Metropolitan Police force, felt it prudent that he, and only he, was in operational control of the whole of the force. He did not get on with his Assistant Commissioner James Monro who, embittered by the frostiness of Warren towards him, resigned his position in August 1888. He was to be replaced by Dr Robert Anderson.

Warren's office as head of the Metropolitan Police was further compromised by the existence within the police force of a secret investigative department that had been created in response to the terrorist threat a number of years before, as Europe burned under revolutionary activity and Britain under the emerging Fenian threat. This department, a secret and self-contained grouping, was known as the Secret Irish Department or Section D. Although operating within the police force, it was answerable to the Home Secretary only. This significantly piqued Warren, for he knew that despite his resignation, Monro was still in charge of this secret department. Even more humiliating for Warren, Monro's secret department had complete power to instruct any member of the force to their aim and instruction without informing Warren. It would also be the case that Warren's Assistant Commissioner, Anderson, was not only a close ally of Monro, but he had also worked deeply in anti-Fenian operations, acting as a control for a network of spies that had infiltrated the various Fenian Brotherhood groups and their many offshoots. In particular, Anderson was the control for an English spy called Thomas Billis Beach, who had successfully penetrated the Fenian movement, avoiding obvious suspicion by claiming to be a French man called Henri Le Caron.

Ireland's domestic situation, both economically and politically, looked bleak as 1888 approached. Such torment would now reach over the Irish Sea. The Irish Republican Brotherhood, an insurgent organisation made up of many competing groups who maintained a fractured unity in the face of the common enemy (Britain), had, since the Irish Famine and the bloody collapse of the nascent nationalist movement Young Ireland in the 1840s, been fermenting this collective discontent into a more radical and violent approach and agenda. Whereas Parnell's pragmatic stance was aimed at winning political independence from Ireland's British overlords, and Michael Davitt, who had previously been a Fenian, now favoured a more radical, direct-action approach that was aimed at a more redistributive political agenda in Ireland, the Fenians – in all their groupings and guises – merely wished to force the British out of Ireland. Their aim was overwhelmingly clear, their methods clearer still; force from the barrel, not so much of the gun, but the powder keg of dynamite! Dynamite was to be their weapon of choice, so much so that they would earn the competing moniker of Dynamitards. Yet it was to be another weapon entirely that would have wider repercussion for Parnell and the Irish in the autumn of 1888: the long-bladed knife.

The murder of Lord Cavendish in Dublin's Phoenix Park in May 1882, on the day of his inauguration as Chief Secretary for Ireland, would have dreadful consequences for the Irish political establishment. He had been appointed by Gladstone, the then Prime Minister. Cavendish had been strolling with his new Permanent Under-Secretary, Thomas Henry Burke, when a number of men pounced on them. This was a deliberate assassination of Cavendish; Burke was an unintended target, but was murdered anyway.

Lord Cavendish, murdered in Phoenix Park, Dublin in May 1882.

The group responsible turned out to be a Irish Republican Brotherhood splinter group known as The Invincibles. The method of dispatch is noteworthy. The two men had been attacked with long thin-bladed knives; surgical knives. Cavendish and Burke had been severely slashed about the abdomen and stabbed. The assassins fled, but many were later apprehended and punished. To Parnell, the activities of the Fenians, although he maintained dialogue with them as much as he could, were a dangerous distraction. He was also aware that certain personalities within his own political groupings, both in Ireland and at Westminster, had strong links or sympathies with the Fenians.

All these anxieties would visit themselves upon Parnell in March 1887 with the a series of articles in *The Times* entitled 'Parnellism & Crime'. As the series continued over subsequent editions, letters purporting to be written by Parnell appeared to show approval for the Phoenix Park murders of Cavendish and Burke. Parnell was traumatised by these revelations, but knew them to be false. After strenuous pressure a Commission was set up – alluded to at the beginning of this piece – to investigate the affair. This Commission would sit during the latter part of the Whitechapel murders, and drag on for another year. By early 1889 it was becoming clear that the calumnious letters implicating Parnell and his political organisations had been forged by a malcontent and dishonest Irish journalist called

Richard Pigott, who committed suicide once he had confessed and been exposed. Interestingly, one of Pigott's providers of information, helping him to construct his letters, was Dr Robert Anderson.

Parnell was eventually cleared by the Commission and successfully sued *The Times* for libel, securing a £5,000 out-of-court settlement and the rehabilitation of his political career and standing. However, the affair had served its purpose to the anti-Irish elements operating both inside and outside the British political establishment. For a critical time the accusations printed in *The Times* had put the IPP off-balance whilst bolstering up support and justification for Balfour's hard line Coercion Act, garnering it greater support. Most importantly, this vilification satisfied and further encouraged those within British society who wished to marginalise, demonise and ultimately destroy Parnell and all his associated political groupings. The result of the Commission's findings by November 1889 might have seen a catharsis for Parnell, but the period going into the Commission had been his nadir. Fenianism stalked Britain in 1888, just as the Whitechapel murderer terrorised the East End. The irony was that the Metropolitan Police force would become embroiled in both. Monro and Anderson's avowed aim was to destroy the Fenians. Monro and Anderson were both of Ulster Protestant stock, and fiercely Unionist in outlook. Throughout the whole of the investigation into the Whitechapel murders, Monro's Section D seemed to take a curious interest in the Fenians as part of its own investigation into the murders. Many detectives were seconded from the wider detective force to act on the orders of Monro. This significantly aggravated already strained relations with Charles Warren who became convinced that Monro's department was misusing their offices in nebulous investigations.

It is not quite clear why Section D should have investigated Fenians

James Monro. His Section D kept documents on many Irish and Fenian suspects as part of an investigation into the Whitechapel murders.

under the scope of the Whitechapel murders. There are three scenarios here: they wished to smear the Fenians with the Whitechapel murders; they believed the Fenians' hand was at work in the murders (especially during the early part of the investigation); or, more feasibly, they were using the intense and sweeping Ripper investigation as a moment of opportunity to investigate Fenians or those suspected of consorting with them. For whatever reason, Monro's Section D kept documents on many Irish/Fenian suspects as part of an investigation into the Whitechapel murders.

Reasons for these overlapping suspicions might be the methods employed by the Fenians in some violent instances such as the murder of Lord Cavendish. The use of a long-bladed surgical knife in this murder and other attacks – such as that by Fenians on Lady Florence Dixie in March 1883 – that used the same weaponry may have put ideas in the sinister minds of those high up in Section D that the Whitechapel murders may have more to them than first appeared.

Ultimately, once the Whitechapel murder investigation progressed, it became abundantly clear that the murderer was a serial killer targeting poor unfortunate women in London's East End. Any prospect of a link to the Fenians was outlandish and unlikely. Even the arrest of a bizarre American by the name of Francis Tumblety at the tail end of 1888 as part of the Whitechapel murder investigation would draw in many detectives involved in the wider investigations of the Fenians and associated groups. The fact that Tumblety may have had tenuous links to the Fenians is a rather interesting angle in this particular affair.

It is intriguing to note that certain sections of the police, especially Melville Macnaghten who joined the Metropolitan Police force as Assistant Chief Constable in 1889, believed that in the late 1880s, the Fenians had embarked on a programme of political assassination. One of the intended victims of these assassination plots seems to have been the Chief Secretary of Ireland, Arthur Balfour. Somehow, Macnaghten convinced himself that this particular plot to kill Balfour was somehow linked to the Whitechapel murders.

The Irish had been victims for years; and 1888 was the year for victims. The mainstream media's portrayal of the Irish was less than complimentary – the satirical magazine *Punch* had made a virtue of the fact that it routinely represented the Irish, and in particular the Hibernian political dimension, to be worthy of dismissive humour that both expressed and reinforced racial stereotypes of the 'dangerous' and 'uncultured' Irish. This was racism in a period that had engendered long-held hostile opinions of foreigners that would be voiced a few years later by the imperialist Cecil Rhodes, who remarked: 'to be born English is to come first in the lottery of life.' Many at the top concurred. After all; was not God an Englishman? Winston Churchill, a Home Ruler himself in his early political career, would put the fraught relationship between the British and the Irish in a darkly pithy comment; 'We have always found the Irish a bit odd. They refuse to be English.' All of Britain's attempts to make and often coerce the Irish into being 'English' would fail. Ultimately, these attempts would push the Irish body politic towards more radical agendas by the early twentieth century. The land of the Gaels and the Celts, of poets, saints and scholars; Ireland was determined on the means of its own destiny.

The prejudice ran deep in the British upper classes in 1888. This, it could be argued, replicated itself in wider society against an ethnic group of which the indigenous population were routinely encouraged to be suspicious and dismissive. The continuing Fenian dynamite outrages during this period did nothing to alleviate this opinion.

The Irish did not suffer in the way the Jews would suffer during the Whitechapel murders. Unlike the Jewish fraternity of the East End, the East End Irish community would not be victims of wild rumours and accusations linking them to the murderous outrages. The Irish community in the East End was significant and influential, and the term 'Irish Cockney' would be used for those Irish, or those of Irish parentage, living in the East End. The docks to the south were famous for this community and an area just north of the Whitechapel Road, known as the 'Fenian Barracks', had a large and noted Irish presence. Yet, the negative effects of the Whitechapel murder investigation would not hit home to the Irish in the way it would hit the Jewish population. For the Irish the effect would be, as we have seen, largely within the political sphere – at least in the early part of the investigation.

By the 1880s the newspaper media had grown to monumental size. The radical titles had also expanded to reach a wider audience. In particular, *The Star* newspaper exemplified the radical press, and the Whitechapel murder series was to prove highly lucrative in increasing sales and readership. The police's failure to apprehend the vile miscreant – although perfectly understandable for various insurmountable reasons – left them open to inevitable criticism from a section of the press who desired to criticise Commissioner Warren for his brutal quelling of Bloody Sunday the previous November. Here was their golden chance. Mockery would be underpinned by intense and longstanding vitriol against the perceived increasing authoritarianism of the police. An audience of the poor, from London and beyond, who were still sceptical of the police force, were easy to indulge in a crisis such as this.

The Irish issue would have played heavy at the back of this wider criticism. Radical elements were favourable to the Irish agenda. Moreover, and vitally, the editor of *The Star* newspaper was T. P. O'Connor. O'Connor was also a Member of Parliament, being a member of Parnell's IPP; he was well able to make sure there was some iron in the glove of criticism against the authorities.

The fact that there were to be elections for the newly formed London County Council in a few months' time also helped galvanise and direct an anti-establishment agenda, as more left-leaning candidates were seeking to be elected. The Whitechapel murders offered them a timely platform to attack their opponents in authority as a form of protesting alliance.

Many years later, James Monro's son Charles would rather enigmatically refer to the investigation of the Whitechapel murders, ascertained from Monro's private papers on the case, as 'a very hot potato'. Of course, the investigation was vexed and complex to a degree that it would have tested the patience of any law enforcement agency, even at its most mundane level. Conspiracy theorists draw all kinds of detail from this statement, to implicate far-reaching involvement by all manner of groups. It would be tempting to see this 'hot potato' statement as referencing a serious accusation against the Fenians, whether correct or otherwise. It would be just as tempting to see a determined attempt to sully the Fenian/Irish political agenda by a Unionist axis in Scotland Yard. The remark may not even refer to the Fenian angle. However, somewhere along the line, certain sections of those controlling the police investigations seemed to see a link to the Fenians, or were determined to link them to the crimes in some way. Ultimately, they would not succeed as the investigation moved in a more conventional direction.

One freezing morning on 9 November 1888, in a lodging room just off the main thoroughfare of Commercial Street, Jack the Ripper found another victim – possibly his last. With the murder of Mary Jane Kelly, in all real likelihood a native from Co. Limerick, Ireland, Jack the Ripper had found his Irish victim.

Adrian Morris

Hailing from Neasden in north-west London, Adrian was born only a stone's throw away from Dollis Hill House where both the great Victorian Prime Minister William Gladstone and the brilliant American writer Mark Twain lived. He studied political science at Birkbeck College, London University and has a long standing interest in Irish history and post-1945 American history. He is a founding member of the Whitechapel Society and is the former editor of its journal.

EIGHT

The Jewish People

By Jacqueline Murphy

The Jewish people of the East End of London were to become victims of Jack the Ripper. To fully understand this it is necessary to look at the history of Jewish settlement in this part of the capital.

Jewish people had settled in London from Roman times, but left in the thirteenth century after King Edward I's edict of expulsion. Gilda O'Neill talks about the origins of the Jewish people in her book *My East End*.

'Although London never had a formalised ghetto as such, the Jewish newcomers were unable to own land in their own right, nor were they able to bear arms. Being visibly different in clothing and customs, they were easily targeted and experienced hostility which at times escalated into mob violence.'

Very few Jews remained, and they practiced their faith secretly until a small group of Sephardi Jews (people originally from Spain or North Africa) were identified. Oliver Cromwell allowed them to remain in England and gradually they were joined by others. In 1753 the Jewish Naturalisation Act was passed, which allowed Jewish people to openly live in England. However, there was great opposition to this bill, and it was repealed the following year. Jewish people were seen as alien and different due to their customs and clothing. They continued to live quietly, and were joined by a different group of Jews, the Ashkenazi, mainly from Amsterdam and Germany. By 1858 there were 25,000 Jews living in London. Both groups of Jews established their own synagogues – The Great Synagogue, originally built in 1690 in Aldgate and rebuilt later several times in Dukes Place, was richly decorated (Benjamin Disraeli worshipped here as a child), whereas the poorer Jews had smaller converted houses or disused Huguenot chapels in which to congregate, such as Sandys Row synagogue and Princelet Street.

As they were not welcomed by Londoners, they made their home in the East End, mainly Whitechapel and Spitalfields, close to the docks. In 1881, Tsar Alexander II was assassinated in St Petersburg. During the aftermath many Jewish people,

Sandy's Row synagogue where the poorer Jews worshipped.

mainly Polish Ashkenazim, were expelled from Russia during a violent pogrom; the assassination was thought, wrongly, to have been organised by the Jews. These people fled and many joined their relatives in London. Some stayed briefly before moving on to America, but others remained permanently, swelling the population to 80,000 in Britain as a whole. Fiona Rule discusses this in her book, *The Worst Street in London.*

'Once admitted to Britain, many of the Eastern European immigrants headed for the East End, mainly because there were established Jewish communities there where they could buy kosher food, speak languages they understood and perhaps even meet up with old friends.'

However, not everyone welcomed these newcomers.

'By the late nineteenth century London's Jewish community had created a niche for itself. Wealthier Jews held office in parliament and were even part of the Royal Family's inner circle. Working class Jews had to work harder than their non-Jewish counterparts to make a living.'

These 'British Jews' believed that these immigrants would undermine their status in society. In 1858 Lionel de Rothschild, a local Jewish man, had been voted into parliament and was allowed to take his seat in the House of Commons even though he would not take 'the offensive' oath, 'by the true faith of a Christian', required by all elected representatives.

This influx stretched resources to the limit. The Jewish people had traditionally looked after their own, and set up schools to help people learn a trade. In the *City Press* dated 23 December 1871 there is a report about a workroom for forty girls to learn 'fancy and plain needlework' run by the Jewish board of Guardians. In 1732 the Jewish Free School was set up, originally in Spitalfields, for orphan boys, and was attached to the Great Synagogue. By 1822 it had to move to larger premises in Bell Lane and by the end of the nineteenth century had 4,000 pupils. The head teacher in 1842 was Moses Angel, and he was keen for the boys to learn English ways in order to assimilate into the local culture. Most local Jewish people spoke a mixture of Hebrew and their own home language, called Yiddish, and this helped to reinforce the alien stereotype as viewed by the indigenous English population. Jewish people saw helping others as their duty. Rachel Lichtenstein, in her book *On Brick Lane*, recalls talking to author William Fishman about his memories of growing up in the area. He said of his grandfather: 'On many occasions I'd walk with him and his immediate response when being stopped by someone less fortunate than himself was to press a handful of coins into their hands with a solemn declaration in the Yiddish vernacular, "Thank you for asking me".'

Fishman himself says that there were many poor Jewish people living in the East End in 1888, 'By 1888 Booth had estimated that of the 40,000 Jews settled in the East End, 15,000 were "quite poor", 15,000 "moderately" so and the remaining 10,000 "comfortably off" or "well off".'

The Jewish Board of Governors set up a temporary shelter in Leman Street to meet people as they got off the boats in order to give them a place to stay, recognising that these people were easy targets for crime. Later, they organised a soup kitchen to feed the growing families of these immigrants, in Brune Street.

Until the 1834 Poor Law Act it was the responsibility of the local parish (church) to give aid to the poor; therefore the Jewish Board of Governors took this responsibility upon themselves, continuing throughout the nineteenth century. Jewish people continued to seek help from their peers rather than go to the workhouse, which led to an increase in animosity from the local non-Jewish population, who had no choice in times of hardship. They saw Jewish people as distant, insular and something to be feared. The Housing Act of 1876 (Artisans and Labourers' Dwelling Act) forced slum landlords to sell their houses to the local councils, who in turn pulled them down in order to build better homes for workers. This led to a shortage of affordable housing and an increasing number of people were forced to live in overcrowded accommodation. The more immigrants arrived and settled in Whitechapel, the more overcrowded the local 'Gentile' (non-Jewish) population became. This inevitably led to resentment. They saw the Jewish people as taking their jobs and homes. This was the general feeling when Jack the Ripper struck in the autumn of 1888.

Although non-Jewish people would often work for Jewish employers, performing duties such as general housework and candle-lighting on a Friday

A Jewish Soup Kitchen, Brune Street.

night, when Orthodox Jews were not permitted to work due to the Sabbath, Jews were still looked upon as being different. Newspapers were full of anti-Semitism. The *Pall Mall Gazette* and *The Star* both reported that human fat was used to make candles in order to induce sleep, and that these candles were used in Russia to help rob people.

It was a difficult time to live in Whitechapel for numerous reasons. The influx of immigrants made housing overcrowded and jobs scarce. In 1886 the *Pall Mall Gazette* had warned its readers that 'the foreign Jews of no nationality whatever are becoming a pest and a menace to the poor native-born East Ender'.

Charles Freak, secretary of the Shoemaker Society said that 'these Jew foreigners work in our trade at this common work sixteen or eighteen hours a day, and the consequence is that they make a lot of cheap and nasty stuff that destroys the market and injures us.'

On 6 October the *East London Advertiser*, discussing the continuing wave of immigrants stated, 'And still they come'. It often had articles vilifying the Jewish population.

The murder of Miriam Angel in Batty Street in 1887 had also highlighted the 'criminality' of the Jews when a fellow lodger, Israel Lipski, was convicted of the crime. Lipski came to be used as a term of derision or insult targeted at those of a Jewish appearance, as can been seen when a witness to the assault of Elizabeth

Stride, Israel Schwartz, was called a 'lipski' as he walked down Berners Street. Schwartz was frightened and ran home. He was later interviewed by the police through an interpreter. *The Star* reported that Schwartz was Hungarian and could not speak a word of English.

It was also reported after the murder of Polly Nicholls that the police were looking for a local man in connection with the murder known as 'Leather Apron'. *The Star* described him as 'a Jewish slipper maker who had abandoned his trade in favour of bullying prostitutes at night'.

The Star newspaper also reported that 'his name nobody knows, but all are united in the belief that he is a Jew or of Jewish parentage, his face being of a marked Hebrew type.'

These views helped foster the belief that 'no Englishman could be capable of such brutal and gruesome crimes'.

Descriptions of the murderer were often interpreted as anti-Semitic.

Israel Lipski convicted of the murder of Miriam Angel in Batty Street in 1887.

Elizabeth Long saw a man talking to Annie Chapman outside 29 Hanbury Street shortly before her death. Long described the man as 'a foreigner' in her inquest testimony.

George Hutchinson gave a very detailed description of a man he saw with Mary Kelly and included the words 'Jewish appearance', as recorded by Philip Sugden in his book *The Complete History of Jack the Ripper*.

The *East London Advertiser* of 15 September 1888 reports that the police were looking for a man who 'spoke with a foreign accent' and that they arrested a man at 9 a.m. the previous Monday in connection with the Whitechapel murders, called John Piser [sic], thought to be known as 'Leather Apron'.

Other men arrested either spoke with an accent or had foreign names, such as Jacob Isenschmit, a butcher, Charles Ludwig, a hairdresser, and Joseph Issacs, a cigar maker, according to Paul Beggs' *The Jack the Ripper A to Z*. All men were later released or incarcerated in an asylum.

Jewish men became wary of being out late at night. As September progressed, there was such a wave of anti-Semitic feeling that mobs began to attack innocent Jews on the streets. The *East London Advertiser* reports that these mobs would shout 'Down with the Jews', and the paper tried to stem the tide of negative feeling. After the 'double event' of 30 September some anti-Jewish graffiti was discovered written in Goulston Street, alongside a piece of apron, later to be proven as belonging to Catharine Eddowes. Due to the mentality of some of the non-Jewish (Gentile) population in the area, Sir Charles Warren ordered that it was erased immediately, a decision which has given countless Ripperologists fuel for discussion ever since. Was Jack the Ripper Jewish? Possibly. However, the local Jewish people were under scrutiny from the police, the press and their neighbours at a time of heightening hysteria.

The Jewish people have always been victims of society. In literature they are seen as evil. Fagin in Dickens' *Oliver Twist*, mercenary Shylock in Shakespeare's *A Merchant of Venice*, or Svengali in George Du Maurier's *Trilby*; the Jews have always had bad press. But they are a resilient race and have always been able to bounce back from persecution; though the worst was yet to come. As well as the press targeting all the Jewish inhabitants of the East End, some individual Jewish people were victims of the mass hysteria surrounding the case; from Piser, suspected of being Leather Apron, to Israel Schwartz, a witness in the wrong place at the wrong time. Two Jewish men caught up in events beyond their control. In countless books written since 1888, many Jewish men have been accused of being Jack the Ripper

But one local man, Aaron Kosminski, was named as possibly being Jack the Ripper by a senior policeman, Sir Melville Macnaghten, as well as in some notes made in a copy of Sir Robert Anderson's biography by Donald Swanson, another policeman. No further evidence is forthcoming. Was Kosminski Jack the Ripper? He was Jewish, so in the eyes of many, that was enough. There can be no doubt that the Jews of the East End were victims of Jack the Ripper.

Bibliography

Books

Begg, Paul, et al, *The Jack the Ripper A to Z*, (Headline, 1991)
Fishman, William, *East End 1888*, (Hanbury, 1988)
Flanders, Judith, *The Invention of Murder*, (Harper, 2011)
Jones, Richard, *Uncovering Jack the Ripper's London*, (New Holland, 2007)
Lichtenstein, Rachel, *On Brick Lane*, (Penguin, 2007)
Mitchell, Sally (ed.), *Victorian Britain: An Encyclopedia*, (St James Press, 1988)
Oldridge, M. W., *Whitechapel and District*, (The History Press, 2011)
O'Neill, Gilda, *My East End*, (Penguin, 1999)
Rule, Fiona, The Worst Street in London, (Ian Allan, 2010)
Sugden, Philip, *The Complete History of Jack the Ripper*, (Robinson, 1994)

Jacqueline Murphy

Jackie lives in Essex and has four grown-up children. She has always been interested in history, but became fascinated by Jack the Ripper after watching the 1973 Barlow and Watt programme as a child. More recently, Jackie has developed two new interests. One is patchwork quilting and the other is travelling. Unfortunately she still has to work to support her interests and is currently a teacher.

NINE

Sir Charles Warren and the Curse of Jack!

By George Fleming

The Essentials ...

Colonel in the Royal Engineers and appointed Commissioner of the Metropolitan Police in March 1886, Sir Charles Warren's tenure of office is generally considered an unhappy one. It coincided with a period of serious social unrest in London, culminating in the Trafalgar Square riots of November 1887. Warren's handling of these has been described as heavy-handed, involving the use of troops and resulting in 150 injuries and one death. His next major crisis was the notorious Jack the Ripper murders. The Met's failure to catch the Ripper and the perceived silliness of some of their attempts have also contributed greatly to Warren's discredit. He finally resigned his office on 9 November 1888, coincidentally the day of the last and worst Ripper murder, and resumed his military career. This terminated during the Boer War, when he was largely blamed for one of the British Army's bloodiest defeats, at the Battle of Spion Kop.

Charles Warren, appointed Commissioner of the Metropolitan Police in March 1886.

But a 'Victim' … ?

At first sight, to call Warren a victim of Jack the Ripper may seem to be stretching the definition a bit far.

Sir Charles was not found lying eviscerated in some dingy London alleyway. He remains one of the few men in 1880s England not suspected of being the ubiquitous Jack! Contrary to popular belief, he didn't lose his job as Superintendent of the Met because he failed to catch our boy.

Yet he has suffered, albeit posthumously, from a loss of reputation almost entirely down to his association with the Whitechapel murders. Had it not been for this, Warren would be a little known footnote in British social and military history. Because of it, he has become widely known and denigrated.

'An Autocratic Soldier … ?'

The first recurring criticism is that it was ludicrous in the first place to put a Regular Army Colonel in charge of the Metropolitan Police. But this is twenty-first-century thinking, which ignores the social landscape of Victorian Britain.

At the risk of stating a cliché, this was a society utterly dominated by social class. Government was in the hands of the aristocracy, the gentry and the upper-middle classes. When Warren took over, the Prime Minister was the Marquess of Salisbury and he, with half of his Cabinet, sat in the House of Lords. The same groups held sway in almost every walk of life. Lesser mortals 'knew their place' and were seriously inhibited in any dealings with their 'betters'.

An effective Police Commissioner had to be able to take on these 'posh boys' confidently and forcefully. To do this, he had to share their social status and have a professional background of total confidence in his own authority. It also helped if he didn't completely depend on them for employment. All of which fitted Colonel Charles Warren to the proverbial 'T'. In fact, we could be describing a typical senior Army officer.

In the 1880s, the Met did not yet have a corps of officers fitted for this top stratum of command. Look at the senior-ranking officers whose names crop up during the Ripper hunt. A minority, like George Littlechild of the Special Branch, were career policemen. The others (Monro and Macnaghten to name a couple) can be described as 'ruling class'.

Now look at the officers who did the actual pursuing: Frederick Abberline; Bill Thick; Walter Dew. All sound 'feet on the pavement' coppers. Good solid men at law enforcement, but hardly the types to stand up to 'top drawer' politicians, like the Marquess of Salisbury, Lord Randolph Churchill, or Warren's *bête noire*, the Home Secretary, Henry Matthews. They were all accustomed to being at the mercy of bosses who could sack them without redress. Not a background that encourages independent thought. Note that when Sir Charles was finally manoeuvred out of his position by Matthews, he wasn't left without a job or pension. He simply resumed the successful military career he knew was waiting for him.

'Mad, Married, or Methodist?'

This raises another point in Warren's favour. He was not a conventional, narrow-minded soldier, but a Royal Engineer; a sapper.

It's hard to overstate the intellectual calibre of the sappers. By the 1880s they were specialists in construction, mapping, railways, telegraph communications and the burgeoning uses of the new-fangled electricity. Before the century was out, they would pioneer motor transportation, aviation and radio. In short, they were the military intelligentsia.

Their rank and file were inevitably of a much higher mental calibre than Rudyard Kipling's earthy Tommies. Literate, articulate technicians, they responded best to officers who combined the conventional military virtues with serious brainpower and imagination.

Engineer officers stood out from the Army's very un-intellectual officer corps. They were regarded by the latter as an odd bunch. Hence the gibe that all sappers were 'mad, married or Methodist' – dodgy qualities to uniformed hearties.

Our man fitted this picture. An experienced Army officer, he had also commanded civilian troops. He had conducted successful diplomacy between white settlers and native tribes in South Africa. He had fought a creditable election campaign as a radical Liberal. He had a serious reputation in Biblical archaeology. He was an Evangelical Christian; a typical mad sapper and formidable all-rounder.

Cerebral as well as military, men like him were in considerable demand in civilian technical fields. For example, the Board of Trade's Railway Inspectorate was almost entirely staffed by seconded or retired Royal Engineer officers. So when the Metropolitan Police ran into real administrative, discipline and morale problems during the 1880s, sappers offered solutions.

Hence Charles Warren's predecessor, Colonel Sir Edmund Henderson, RE., and Warren himself. Both would have found policemen not unlike the soldiers they had commanded, and the Met's problems easily recognisable as the results of poor officering, chaotic administration and failure to address morale factors in the ranks; all familiar concepts.

New Broom (with bristles!) ...

Warren carried out the two jobs he had been brought in to do.

First was reform of the force. When he took over, morale was low because of poor service conditions, and its inefficiency had become a bad joke. By the time he quit, he had sorted most of this out and, indeed, is sometimes credited with being the creator of the modern Met.

He was less successful with the chaotic administration and endemic empire-building by department heads, like Monro of the CID. Here, he was not supported by the insipid Home Secretary, Henry Matthews, who allowed department heads to deal directly with the Home Office. Warren had some successes, however. The CID was brought under his control, but undisciplined disruption of the chain of command was infuriating to an able professional soldier and brought out the negative side of Warren's character. He did not suffer fools gladly, he had an irascible temper and he tended to act impulsively; in fact, he was something of a prima donna.

This led him into repeated confrontations. Finally, he wrote a critical article in *Murray's Magazine* without clearing it in advance with Matthews. This was (and still is) a breach of public service protocol. In the resultant spat with the Home Office, Warren behaved in character and 'flounced from the stage'.

Now, if his police career had simply amounted to this, he would have gone down in history as a reforming Commissioner of the Met and probably an important influence on British policing generally. However, he would not have become widely known, outside a limited circle of police historians.

But now his story attracts the attention of the Ripper industry ...

Bloodless Sunday ...

Even his success in stopping the riots of 1887 would merely be mentioned in passing by social historians and laboured by social polemicists.

But in the field of serious Ripperology and amongst dabblers in this black art, it is a commonplace that there was appalling mass poverty and homelessness in London's East End. This led first of all to major demonstrations in Trafalgar Square, which Warren first tried to prohibit and then disperse by force.

To compound his wickedness, he actually turned loose troops from the Guards and Household Cavalry, in addition to his 4,000 policemen.

The climax of this confrontational approach was the rioting in Trafalgar Square; on Sunday 13 November, which was dispersed with a total of 150 injured and one man actually dead. This was immediately christened Bloody Sunday by the anti-Government press, and the term has come down to us as an indelible stain on Warren's reputation.

But how 'bloody' was it?

In 1819, troops killed eleven people and injured another 500 or so in Manchester, dispersing an entirely peaceful mass meeting. In 1839 the Army shot dead twenty-two Welsh Chartists during the so-called 'Newport Rising'. Although Britain had a deep-rooted aversion to the use of military force against civil unrest, there was nevertheless a steady trickle of killings throughout the nineteenth century. Compared with our continental opposite numbers, we were the merest amateurs.

In France, where admittedly things tended to get out of hand, 496 Parisians were killed in the rioting which led to the 1830 revolution. In Russia, in January 1905, a peaceful demonstration was fired on by troops and 200 men, women and children killed. This list could be expanded almost ad lib. Warren's 'Bloody Sunday' compares favourably with similar situations in Britain, and would scarcely have raised an eyebrow in Paris or St Petersburg.

As for the use of soldiers, it was, and still remains, one of the Army's constitutional duties to act in support of the civil power when it loses control of public order. Thankfully, this is no longer commonplace in the mainland United Kingdom.

In Victorian Britain it was commonplace, because the police did not have the specialist training or equipment of a modern force. They also lacked the 'force multipliers' of helicopters, radio, and personnel carriers. So there was nothing in the least sinister in Warren having a strong military backup on hand in Trafalgar Square. What is significant, though, is that he restrained the troops from overreacting with a volley or a bayonet charge.

The rioting in Trafalgar Square on Sunday 13 November 1887 was immediately christened 'Bloody Sunday'.

An Enemy of the People ... ?

Warren's role in suppressing the demonstrations led to a campaign of vilification against him, from the political opposition, the radical press and, of course, those who had been actively engaged. In the East End, his name was an anathema. This was completely predictable and it is unlikely he lost any sleep over it. Even today it's the sort of thing a senior police officer has to learn to live with.

But in fact the Government, most of the press and probably most of the British public actually approved. It may surprise devotees of its history, but the East End was not Britain. It was not even London! The majority of Londoners, of all social classes, might sympathise with the East Enders in their misery, but they didn't want London turned into a bear garden every other weekend. Very few people in Great Britain wanted revolution.

Since the coming of universal education in the 1870s, schoolbooks had taught the masses about the bloodbath of the French Revolution. Not just powdered aristocrats, but thousands, of all classes, going to the guillotine. Tens of thousands purged overall. The French still hadn't got it right! The British press had described more recent horrors unleashed in Paris by the revolutions of 1830, 1848 and 1871.

By the last decades of the nineteenth century, the popular consensus in Britain was in favour of political evolution and against violent change – especially violent change inspired by hot-headed foreigners. Morris Eagle, Isaac Kozebrodsky and their fellow enthusiasts at the Berner Street political club were not popular East End figures.

In November 1887, regardless of their views on East End poverty, many people felt that they were seeing a mob of desperate sans-culottes, abetted by groups clearly out for violent criminality and dodgy-looking foreign types shouting weird political slogans and singing (of all things) 'La Marseillaise'. Most were rather glad when Warren's crushers put a stop to it.

This is why it was politically possible to appoint him a Knight Commander of the Order of the Bath and promote him rapidly in his resumed Army career, even after his acrimonious split with the Home Office.

So why is Warren still routinely vilified, and why is this so widespread?

Victim Number 1 ...?

Most of it stems from Warren's involvement with the Ripper murders a year later.

The dire conditions of the East End are the very stuff of the Ripper story. You can't read about Jack without learning about the human degradation that led to the protests and riots. It's very difficult to read about it without feeling real anger, pity and empathy for the East Enders.

Against this backdrop, the wider picture is ignored. The scenario is one where pitiful human beings appeal for help and are brutalised by Warren, the 'fat cats' hired enforcer, and his uniformed thugs. Warren, the police villain who couldn't stop a real villain a year later!

Suppose Jack had plied his trade elsewhere (say in Liverpool) and the local Chief Constable's heavies had cracked a few Scouse skulls; might we not hear a lot less about Warren and Trafalgar Square?

So how did his involvement with the Ripper lead him into history's line of fire?

The Real Victims …

The Ripper murders are generally held to have begun with the slaughter of Polly Nichols, in Buck's Row, on the night of 30 August 1888. During the following weeks he claimed three more victims – Annie Chapman, Elizabeth Stride and Catherine Eddowes. Finally, on 8 November, came the final and most horrific slaying; that of Mary Kelly. This was the full extent of his 'Autumn of Terror'.

Or was it?

Throughout time, doubts have been raised as to whether these five women were his total score and, indeed, whether they were all Ripper victims. Thus, there are arguments that Elizabeth Stride was simply the target of random violence. Mary Kelly may have been killed by another pervert, whose methods even Jack might have considered excessive.

At the same time, there are those who argue that other murdered women, notably Martha Tabram, should be added to the list. So, among Ripperologists, the convention has grown up that the five listed above should be 'taken as read', while leaving the door open for other suggestions. They have therefore become known as 'the canonical five'.

The relevance of all this is that it illustrates the near impossibility of Warren's identifying the Ripper by any process of analysis or deduction. Since August 1888, many very good minds have wrestled with the problem, as well as a throng of enthusiasts, and we are really no further forward.

I have mentioned modern 'force multipliers', in relation to public disorder. For serial killings add CCTV cameras, DNA analysis, computerised records etc. None of these were even remotely available in the 1880s.

Two later police standbys were also lacking. Fingerprinting would not come in for another thirteen years, and the only thing pathologists could tell from blood was how old it might be and whether it came from a mammal. So even finding bloodstained garments indicated no more than a possibility; given the amount of blood routinely visible in the East End, it would have been no more than a workable possibility.

If Jack was going to have his astrakhan collar felt, he would have to be caught red-handed, by entrapment, by finding seriously incriminating items on him, or from information received.

This explains Warren's methodology. He flooded the East End, day and night, with policemen, both uniformed and in plain clothes. He launched a house-to-house search of hundreds of dwellings. Surprisingly, in view of his Bloody Sunday unpopularity, this was accepted placidly. An unusual amount of information was also volunteered by the public. Clearly fear of the Ripper overcame their normal reluctance to 'grass'.

Some of his methods provoked mirth in the popular press; for example, having constables patrol the streets with bits of rubber tied to the soles of their boots, and dressing some as women to act as decoys. Curiously, these are still sometimes seen as amusing.

One wonders at this. In the era of hobnailed boots, Jack would have heard a constable coming a mile away. In fact, it was almost a principle of British policing that the police should be seen and heard. Good for civil liberties, but not so good for surprising a back-alley murderer.

Reading about the 'Old Bill' in drag, most of us probably imagine Dixon of Dock Green trying to look like Barbara Windsor. But the prostitutes of 1888 did not, generally speaking, look like the delightful Babs playing a Ripper victim, in colourful velvet and feathers. The women were often dumpy and bloated, due to cheap alcohol and sickness. They would wear two, sometimes three, layers of clothing, and often

Charles Warren inspects the chalked message in Goulston Street.

men's jackets and boots. It would not be difficult to make a younger policeman look like one of these shapeless lumps, especially if he'd 'got a jolly bonnet', like poor Polly Nichols on her last sortie.

Warren was guilty of a bêtise when he tried out the possible use of bloodhounds, by having a pair chase him through Hyde Park. It didn't help that the sad-faced canines were called Burgho and Barnaby! But the bloodhound idea wasn't his. It came from the Home Office, and he was opposed to it because hounds were ineffective in a crowded urban environment. The trial was a loyal, perhaps impetuous, attempt to evaluate his boss's suggestion.

Acting as the quarry was simply a misjudgement on how it would be treated in the (by then) hostile press.

His other notorious mistake was ordering the erasing of the chalked message in Goulston Street, which may have been scrawled by the Ripper. Whether it was remains a subject of debate, as does the likely usefulness of an 1880's vintage photograph. But at that stage in the murders, the Police couldn't afford to treat any evidence that casually.

Warren's justification was the graffito's reference to 'Juwes' and the possibility that it might lead, within an hour of its discovery, to a pogrom against the Jewish immigrants in the East End. He remained proud for the rest of his life that, throughout the Ripper crisis, he had protected the Jewish community from the anti-Semitic bigotry it aroused and that he had earned a letter of thanks from the Chief Rabbi; strange for an alleged establishment brute!

The speed with which he erased the message probably had a lot to do with his impetuosity, already noted, and tendency to 'shoot from the hip' when beset with argument. Disappointing for conspiracy theorists though!

All of this has reappeared often since, in criticism of Warren. At the time, the main effect of failure to catch the Ripper was that it lost him the support he had actually gained over Bloody Sunday and made him vulnerable in his dealings with the Home Office and his opponents in the Met. Does this class him as a 'real', as opposed to 'historical' victim? The final stage in his career certainly makes him one ...

'The Model of a Modern Major General ...'

As I have said earlier, after his resignation, Warren's military career resumed as normal.

Far from being damaged by Bloody Sunday or the Whitechapel murders, he actually prospered. In 1888 he was appointed Knight Commander of the Order of the Bath. In 1897, he was promoted Lieutenant General – three ranks up from 1888, and only one down from the very top rank of Field Marshal. His place in the *Dictionary of National Biography* was now assured. He would figure as an able contributor to Victorian military history. But he would be unspectacular, outside the Whitechapel affair.

To become really famous, a military man had to be a successful commander in battle, and all Victorian military men dreamt of this. Warren's big chance came in 1899, with the outbreak of the South African (or Second Boer) War. And, sadly, he muffed it.

The Dutch-South African enemy looked like easy meat. These 50,000 undisciplined farmers should have been no match for the highly professional British Army of 250,000. But the Boers handed the Army a whole series of humiliating defeats, and Warren was caught up in one of these.

His performance was inept. He was prey to indecision, he moved sluggishly, and he failed to exploit initiatives created by subordinates. Finally, he attacked and occupied a hill called Spion Kop without proper reconnaissance. His horrified infantry then found Boer riflemen on higher hills; they were trapped in a killing ground. Spion Kop was to go down in history as one of the British Army's stupidest defeats, with 1,700 soldiers lost. Warren was primarily responsible and he was scapegoated. He was to be one of the many inept generals who lost their names in that war.

The trouble was that he and his colleagues were very good at what they were mostly required to do; that is, fighting enemies who were culturally unable to adapt to modern weaponry. Sudanese, Zulus, and Afghans were all brave, efficient fighters, capable occasionally of beating the British in pitched battles. But they could never win in the long haul, because they simply couldn't get their heads around modern firepower tactics, even when they had the firepower.

The Boers had excellent modern rifles, machine guns, barbed wire and even some modern artillery. The result was a sad procession of British generals, like Warren, who couldn't get their heads round really modern firepower tactics.

'Canonical Victim No 6 ... ?'

How many people today have heard of Colley ... Gatacre ... Buller ... Butler ... Methuen ... or the many others in that melancholy throng? Outside a few dedicated military enthusiasts, they are mercifully concealed from our gaze.

Like his hard-nosed approach to public order on Bloody Sunday, poor Warren's military failure has been exposed to many because it is mentioned in so many Ripper studies.

Victimhood

So here is the heart of the matter. Warren had an outstanding military career, until Spion Kop. As Metropolitan Police Commissioner, he successfully discharged his two main duties – reforming the force and pacifying London – without serious bloodshed. But to most of us he would be virtually unknown, had he not been centre stage in the great Whitechapel mystery.

He had the mischance to be a high-profile player in the ongoing Jack the Ripper show, which, like the famous Windmill Theatre, never closes.

Bibliography

Books

Begg, Paul, Fido, Martin, and Skinner, Keith, *The Jack the Ripper A to Z* (Headline, 1996)

Evans, Stewart P., & Rumbelow, Don, *Jack the Ripper: Scotland Yard Investigates*, (The History Press, 2010)

Warren, Charles, *Underground Jerusalem: an account of some of the principal difficulties encountered in its exploration and the results obtained. With a narrative of an expedition through Jordan Valley and a visit to the Samaritans* (Ulan Press, 2012)

Williams, Watkins W., *Life of General Sir Charles Warren* (Blackwell, 1941)

George Fleming

George hails from Scotland and is a graduate in history from Edinburgh University. His Army career, in the R.A.E.C. brought him to Salisbury, Wiltshire in 1976 where he still resides. He writes historical documentaries for live performance by his own group – 'History at Large' – and he has given several well received presentations to the Whitechapel Society.

TEN

Innocent
(and Not So Innocent)
Bystanders

By Ted Ball

The murder of Mary Ann Nichols on 31 August 1888 was reported in the newspapers, but caused little public reaction until *The Star*, on 4 September mentioned a man with the nickname 'Leather Apron' and, the following day, published a feature claiming that 'Leather Apron' had been terrorising the prostitutes of the East End for some time. They gave a detailed description of the man, supposedly based on interviews with fifty women. Although this story is today believed by many to be an invention by a *The Star* reporter, it was taken up by other papers at the time and spread rapidly. The murder of Annie Chapman on 8 September, just a few days later, was widely reported in the newspapers along with innumerable wild rumours, groundless accusations and stories of panic in the East End.

The Times, on Monday 10 September reported:

> On Saturday and yesterday several persons were detained at the various police stations in the district, but were liberated after proper inquiries had been made; and up to the present time the police have no clue to the murderer and lament that they have no good ground to work upon ... So many stories of 'suspicious' incidents have cropped up since the murder, some of them evidently spontaneously generated by frantic terror, and some, even where credible, pointing in contrary directions that it would be idle to refer to them.

On the same day *The Times* also reported a rumour that the murderer had been caught, which turned out to be based on the arrest of a blind man in Spitalfields Market on an unconnected charge; a woman accosted by a man who offered two brass medals as half-sovereigns, (although her description of him did not match that of 'Leather Apron'); a woman who went to the Queen's Head pub with a man who, she noticed, had a large knife in his pocket and whose description was 'Identical with Leather Apron' and a man reported to the police on the Saturday evening by a newsagent in Deptford as having entered the shop in an excited state, being so eager to get hold of a newspaper with an account of the Whitechapel Murder that, on being told there were none left, he snatched the paper the newsagent was reading and ran off.

In the following days a number of men were identified as 'Leather Apron', the best known being John Pizer, a bootmaker who was arrested on 10 September by Sergeant Thick, but was released on 11 September after providing alibis for the times of the murders of Nicholls and Chapman. It was

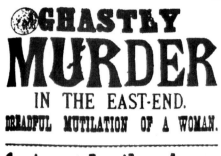

The famous Leather Apron Poster.

later reported that he had been compensated by the newspapers for labelling him the Whitechapel murderer, although the only definite payment he received was a relatively small amount from *The Star* in an out-of-court settlement that saved the newspaper from an expensive libel suit.

The newspapers frequently referred to the killer as a 'lunatic', 'madman', or 'maniac'. In two cases that were widely reported at the height of the Leather Apron scare, the only grounds for suspicion seem to be that the suspect had mental health problems.

Jacob Isenschmidt, a butcher living in Holloway, North London, suffered from delusions and hallucinations, and had frequently threatened to kill members of his family and his neighbours. He had been in Colney Hatch asylum from 24 September to 2 December 1887, and on 11 September 1888, two doctors informed the police that they believed he was the Whitechapel murderer. Isenschmidt was taken to Holloway police station on 12 September. After medical examination he was declared to be of 'unsound mind' and was sent first to the local workhouse infirmary and later to an asylum at Bow.

Another case that received considerable press coverage was that of William Henry Pigott. He was born in 1835, the son of an insurance agent. At one time Pigott had owned a pub in Hoxton, and later worked in several pubs. On 8 June 1888 he was admitted to Whitechapel Infirmary suffering from alcoholism, where he gave his occupation as ship's cook. He was released on 30 July.

On Sunday 9 September in the Pope's Head public house in Gravesend, bloodstains on his clothing and his hostile remarks directed towards women drew a great deal of attention. The landlady of the pub sent for the police, and Pigott was arrested and taken to Whitechapel where he was greeted by a large crowd outside Commercial Street police station. Pigott was shown to several women who the police thought able to recognise the murderer, but they all said he was not 'Leather Apron'.

Pigott had been acting in an increasingly strange manner and becoming incoherent. The divisional surgeon examined him and issued a certificate to the effect that 'the prisoner's mind was unhinged', and Pigott was transferred to the Whitechapel Infirmary on 10 September. The police soon satisfied themselves that Pigott had no connection with the murders, but due to his alcoholism he was held in the Whitechapel Infirmary until 9 October. All that seems to be known about him after this is that he died in 1901.

The case of Julius Lipman is an interesting one. Nothing appears to have been reported of him at the time, but on Saturday October 20, 1900, The *Hampshire Telegraph* and *Naval Chronicle* both printed a brief obituary under the headline 'Not Jack the Ripper':

> A man named Julius Lipman has just died in the East End of drink, neglect and starvation. He was a cobbler by trade, and was known as 'Leather Apron.' He fell under the suspicion of being Jack the Ripper, and although he completely proved his innocence the stigma never quite left him, and his business dwindled away. Lipman was peculiarly unfortunate in the matter. 'Leather Apron' as a possible Jack the Ripper was invented by an imaginative journalist on a sensational paper. He did not suspect for a moment that there was a real man in the district known by that name.

Unfounded accusations made for trivial reasons were common throughout the 1888.

On 18 September *The Times* reported the case of Edward Quinn, a labourer, who appeared at Woolwich police court, 'charged nominally with being drunk at the police-station'. Quinn made a complaint to the court, denying that he was drunk, and saying that after cutting his face and hands in a fall in the street near Woolwich Arsenal, he had gone to a bar where a man gave him beer and tobacco and then took him to the police station, where he was charged with the Whitechapel murders. The magistrate first ordered that Quinn should be remanded in custody, but when Quinn objected released him on bail. There seems to have been no reason for suspecting him other than the blood on his face and hand; and the killer would surely not have had fresh wounds two weeks after the murder of Annie Chapman.

Two incidents apparently generated by the panic that followed the murder of Mary Kelly were reported in *The Times* on 15 November. An off-duty City police

"JACK THE RIPPER" MEMORIES.

Death of "Leather Apron."

The death has occurred in the East End of Julius Lipman, nicknamed "Leather Apron," a cobbler who in 1899 fell under suspicion of being "Jack the Ripper." He satisfied the police of his innocence, but the stigma never left him. His business gradually disappeared, and he went to another neighbourhood, where he took to drink. He died of neglect and semi-starvation.

The stigma of being named as Jack the Ripper left Julius Lipton a broken man.

constable in civilian clothes 'wearing a low broad-brim hat of rather singular appearance' was walking along Commercial Road when several people called out that he was Jack the Ripper. He tried to escape but was followed by the mob, and had to be rescued by uniformed constables from H Division, to whom he was able to identify himself. In the second incident, a man stared into the face of a woman, who screamed that he was Jack the Ripper. He was quickly surrounded by a crowd. Rescued by the police, he was taken to Commercial Street police station, where he was able to satisfy them that he was from Germany and had only arrived in London on the Tuesday.

Although the fear and panic caused by the Ripper murders may have been exacerbated by the overly imaginative and sensational reporting from some sections of the Press, newspapermen were not immune from the suspicions of the public or the attentions of the police. A sixteen-page booklet, *The Whitechapel Atrocities: Arrest of a Newspaper Reporter*, published in 1888 and reprinted in 1999 by Andy Aliffe, recounts the hostile reception accorded to one investigator in the East End. The anonymous author begins:

Of the many men who have been arrested on suspicion of being the perpetrator of the Whitechapel murders, or of having some connection with these terrible crimes, no one's case, perhaps, is more suitable than my own to illustrate the foolish and shallow evidence upon which so many transparently innocent persons have been detained by the police and temporarily incarcerated. Among the large number of individuals who have had to suffer the shame and ignominy of being marched to a police-station, followed by a howling mob, threatening – and in some cases carrying out their threats to a certain extent – to take the law into their own hands, and 'lynch 'im', I stand unique, in one respect at least. I am, I believe, up to the present time, the only person who has had to pass through this dangerous ordeal twice, and that in one day.

The author spent the four nights up to Saturday 24 November in Spitalfields and Whitechapel seeking information on the life of the inhabitants of the area, and before describing his arrests, tells of two earlier terrifying incidents.

Many men were arrested on suspicion of being the perpetrator of the Whitechapel murders.

On the Wednesday night he encountered in a pub 'a black-visaged, thick-set, desperate fellow, with a savage look in his dark eyes', who first described a number of historical murders and then claimed to be Jack the Ripper. The reporter eventually managed to slip out of the pub, and returned with two plain clothes police officers. The man had left by that time but the bar staff confirmed the story, and the reporter made a statement at Leman Street police station. A search was made for the man but he was never found.

After spending the Friday night in the neighbourhood, the reporter was standing at a coffee stall at about 2 a.m. that morning, where he got into conversation with an 'unfortunate', for whom he bought a piece of cake. On leaving the stall he was followed by three youths who had been eavesdropping, and who, he was told later, were criminals. They spoke with him about Jack the Ripper and at length claimed that there were grounds for suspecting him. They then called a policeman, who dismissed their accusation and sent them off.

Not deterred by these experiences, the reporter went into a pub in Commercial Street between six and seven that morning. The men and women drinking there immediately began talking about him and a young man asked his opinion about the murders. Thinking the reply suspicious, the young man left the pub and returned with a uniformed police constable, described by the reporter as 'one of the youngest and most inexperienced-looking that I have seen', who questioned him and spoke with others in the pub. The constable then took the reporter outside and called two other officers, who told him to ignore the accusations and release the reporter. The young constable disregarded their advice and took the reporter to Leman Street police station, followed by a yelling crowd. At the station the accusers were interviewed by an inspector; despite their protests they were dismissed, and the reporter released.

Still undeterred, the reporter took two friends on a tour of the murder sites on the Saturday night. After his friends had left, he went into a large, crowded pub near Dorset Street. He soon began speaking to a man at the bar, and the conversation quickly turned to the subject of the murders. A remark was made by an Irish woman that he was Jack the Ripper. His reply to the effect that it was not the first time he had been mistaken for the Ripper confirmed the suspicions of two 'amateur detectives', who took him outside and handed him over to a policeman who took him to Commercial Street police station, accompanied by a drunken mob. He was interrogated by the superintendent and by the detectives in charge of the Ripper investigation, who had been summoned for the purpose, and also asked to account for his movements on the night of Mary Kelly's murder. His protestations of innocence were eventually believed, and he was escorted home by two police officers.

Another incident involving a journalist was reported in the *Sussex Daily News* on 23 November 1888:

For a philanthropist to find himself charged with being drunk and disorderly is a disagreeable experience. Mr. W.S. Ralston has been interesting himself very humanely in the relief of the distressed Russian singers, who seem to have come to the country with very primitive ideas of business. But in the midst of this benevolent work Mr. Ralston suddenly finds himself charged at Bow-street with drunkenness. He had gone to a police-station at midnight, and, according to a constable, had asked for the Home Secretary. The constable remarked that Mr. Matthews did not live there, and advised Mr. Ralston to go away; whereupon Mr. Ralston used abusive language. His explanation was that he had been in Whitechapel with a member of the Russian Embassy, and that his business as a journalist took him to police-stations at all hours. He wanted some assistance from the police, and finding them needlessly suspicious, he mentioned the Home Secretary and other exalted persons as his friends. Upon this they took him into custody. The incident is mysterious, but the minds of the police are rather excited just now, and we suppose that a man who goes to a police-station in the middle of the night, and says that he knows Mr. Matthews and Sir William Harcourt, may seem an undesirable citizen to be left at large. The tactics of the Whitechapel murderer have deranged the official mind; and no policeman would be in the least surprised if the monster were to claim acquaintance with the Queen. Something of that kind is evidently what criminals are now expected to do; and Mr. Ralston and other amateur investigators who roam about at night must expect to be locked up the moment they mention any of their friends. The magistrate suggested that Mr. Ralston should avoid police-stations in future; and to this counsel we would add the suggestion that until the Whitechapel mystery is solved, no citizen should mention in a constable's hearing anybody more important than a chimney sweep.

One misadventure of the anonymous author of *The Whitechapel Atrocities* was being reported to a constable as Jack the Ripper by the three youths at the coffee stall; this was no doubt intended as a prank and was not the only such accusation made by drunks (or by a group of those young people who seem unable to find anything to amuse themselves beyond hanging about in the street and harassing innocent passers-by).

On 15 October 1888 *The Times* published a long letter, signed 'An Elderly Gentleman'. The writer describes how, when out in one of the mining districts, he was approached by a group of seven young people, most appearing to be about eighteen years old, who accused him of being Jack the Ripper. Their leader claimed to be a constable with a warrant and would either take him to the police station, or shoot him. The gentleman called to another man who was approaching for assistance and the two of them walked off, followed by the group of youths, eventually reaching the safety of the home of a friend of the gentleman.

On 13 November *The Times* reported a case at Marlborough Street police court, where William Avenell and Frederick W. Moore were charged with being disorderly and assaulting Henry Edward Leeke on the previous Saturday. Leeke went into a pub at about 5 p.m. and was accosted by several men, who said that they were detectives and were arresting him as Jack the Ripper. They took him outside, beat him and questioned him. Being told that he had just delivered some oil to 62 Berner Street, they dragged him there, where he managed to get away from them and run into the basement, where some young women were having tea. Avenell followed him and after finding Leeke hiding in the cellar, again claimed to be a private detective and that Leeke was Jack the Ripper. The landlady recognised Leeke, who made regular deliveries there, and sent for a constable who arrested Avenell and Moore.

Other drunks found themselves in court after frightening people by pretending to be Jack the Ripper. On 14 November *The Times* reported that a man named Avery, who had been drinking, seized a man in the street as a practical joke, saying 'I'm Jack the Ripper and this is how I do it', and running his hands up the front of the victim's clothes. A similar case was reported on 16 November. John Benjamin Perriman was charged with being drunk and disorderly on the Old Kent Road. He had declared himself to be Jack the Ripper, flourished a black leather bag, and caught hold of several women. He was soon surrounded by an angry crowd and had to be rescued by the police, who took him to the station, followed by the excited mob.

These are just a few of the 'innocents' who were caught up in the Autumn of Terror. All of them are long gone, but their posthumous reputations are victims of Jack the Ripper.

Bibliography

Books

Anon, *The Whitechapel Atrocities: Arrest of a Newspaper Reporter* (1888)

Newspapers

Hampshire Telegraph, 20 October 1900
Naval Chronicle, 20 October 1900
Sussex Daily News, 23 November 1888
The Star, 4 September 1888
The Times, 10 September 1888, 18 September 1888, 15 October 1888, 13-16 November 1888

Ted Ball

Ted is a valued member of the Whitechapel Society and he has been involved with the organisation since 1998. A retired bookseller, Ted has been interested in Jack the Ripper and London's East End for over forty years. He has a large collection of rare books relating to Ripper studies and has contributed articles to all the leading magazines on the subject of Jack the Ripper.

If you enjoyed this book, you may also be interested in...

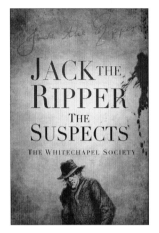

Jack the Ripper: The Suspects
THE WHITECHAPEL SOCIETY

Jack the Ripper has baffled the authorities for centuries. Just who was responsible for the gruesome murders that rocked Victorian London?

Each member of The Whitechapel Society has spent many years researching the topic and the results of their latest, cutting-edge investigations are published here for the first time.

With each chapter discussing a separate suspect in detail, this book is the ultimate guide to the most famous criminal investigation in British history.

9780752462868

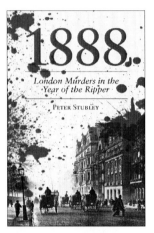

1888: London Murders in the Year of the Ripper
PETER STUBLEY

What was London like in 1888? The infamous Jack the Ripper murders made the headlines and remain a source of fascination to this day, but what of the murders committed by ordinary citizens? What drove them to commit such terrible acts? Using old crime records, Peter Stubley builds a picture of a contemporary society shaped by desperate circumstances.

Written by a renowned crime journalist, this book gives avoice to the forgotten victims of 1888.

9780752465432

Abberline: The Man Who Hunted Jack the Ripper
PETER THURGOOD

Frederick George Abberline is synonymous with Jack the Ripper, but his story goes far beyond the events of 1888. A dedicated policeman in a time of extraordinary corruption, Abberline was behind some of the most famous investigations in criminal history, from the Cleveland Street Scandal to infiltrating the Fenian terrorist group.

This book charts his extraordinary rise through the ranks of the Metropolitan Police and his life away from the force – a very different man to that portrayed in the media.

9780752488103

Visit our website and discover thousands of other History Press books.

www.thehistorypress.co.uk